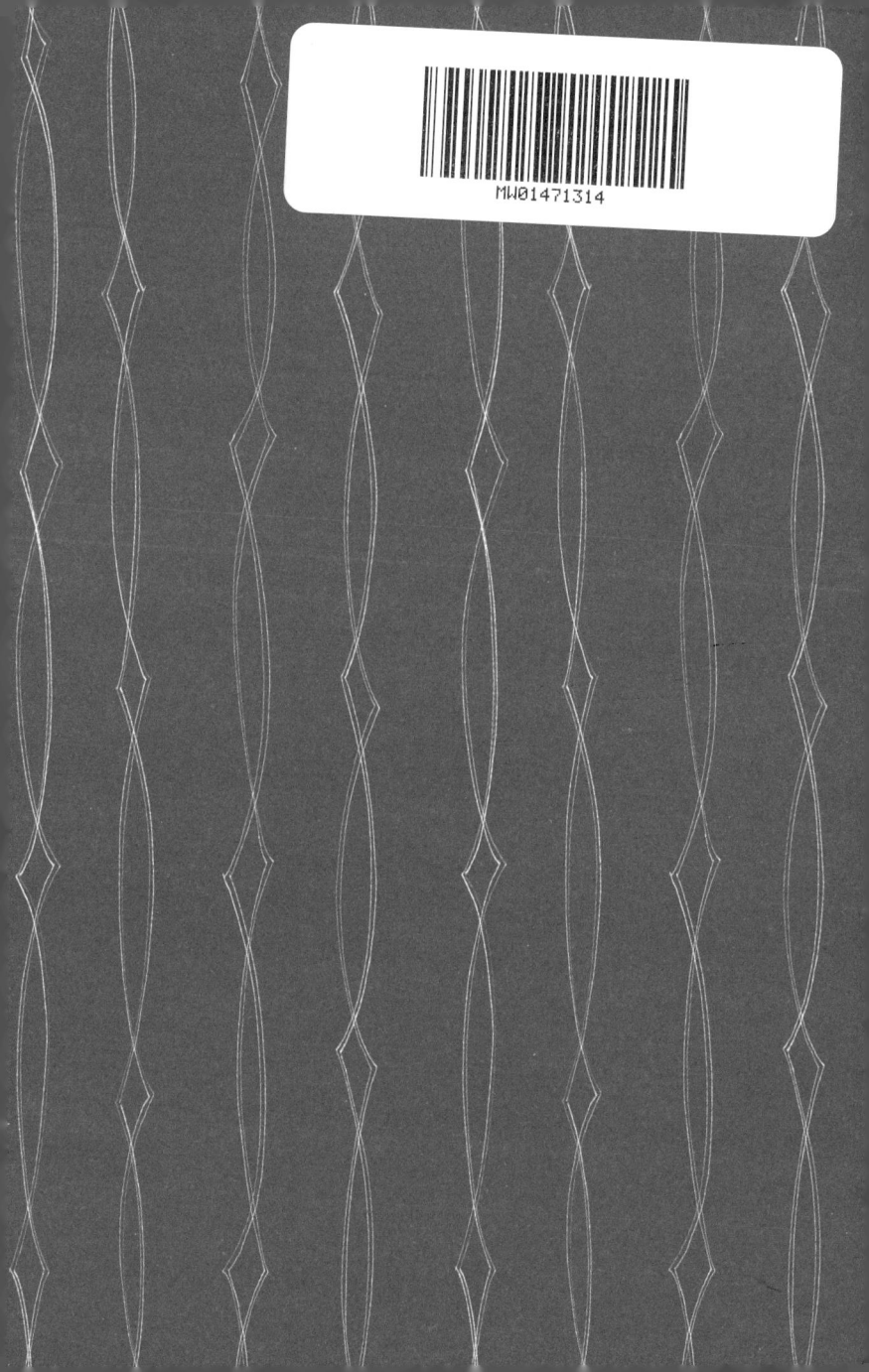

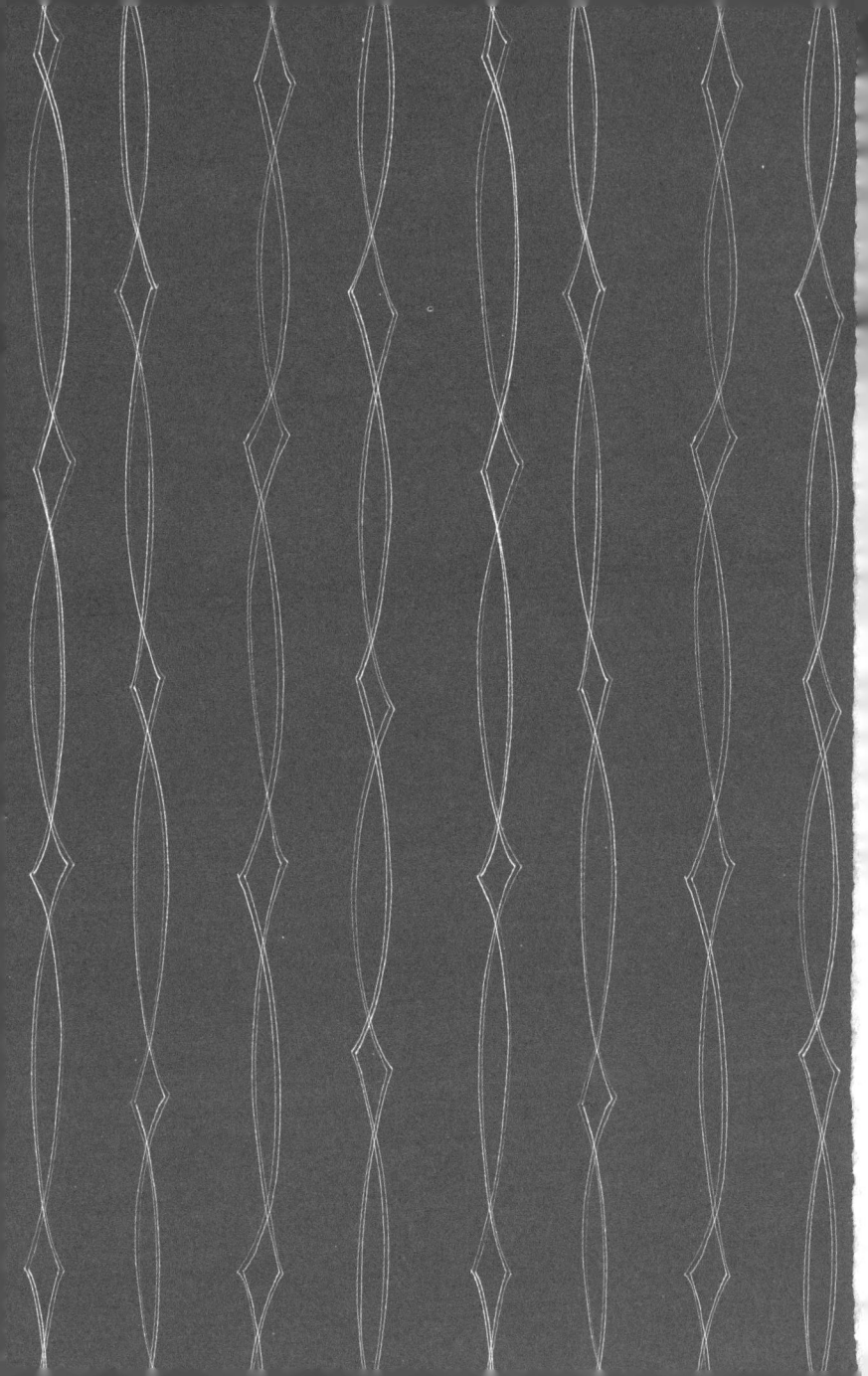

COWBOY BOOTS
THE ART & SOLE

COWBOY BOOTS
THE ART & SOLE

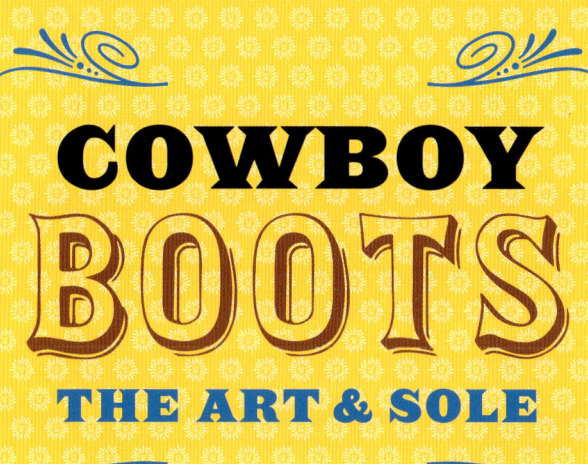

Jennifer June

PHOTOGRAPHS BY Marty Snortum

FOREWORD BY Dwight Yoakam

UNIVERSE

"Roy Rogers."
Rocketbuster vintage collection.

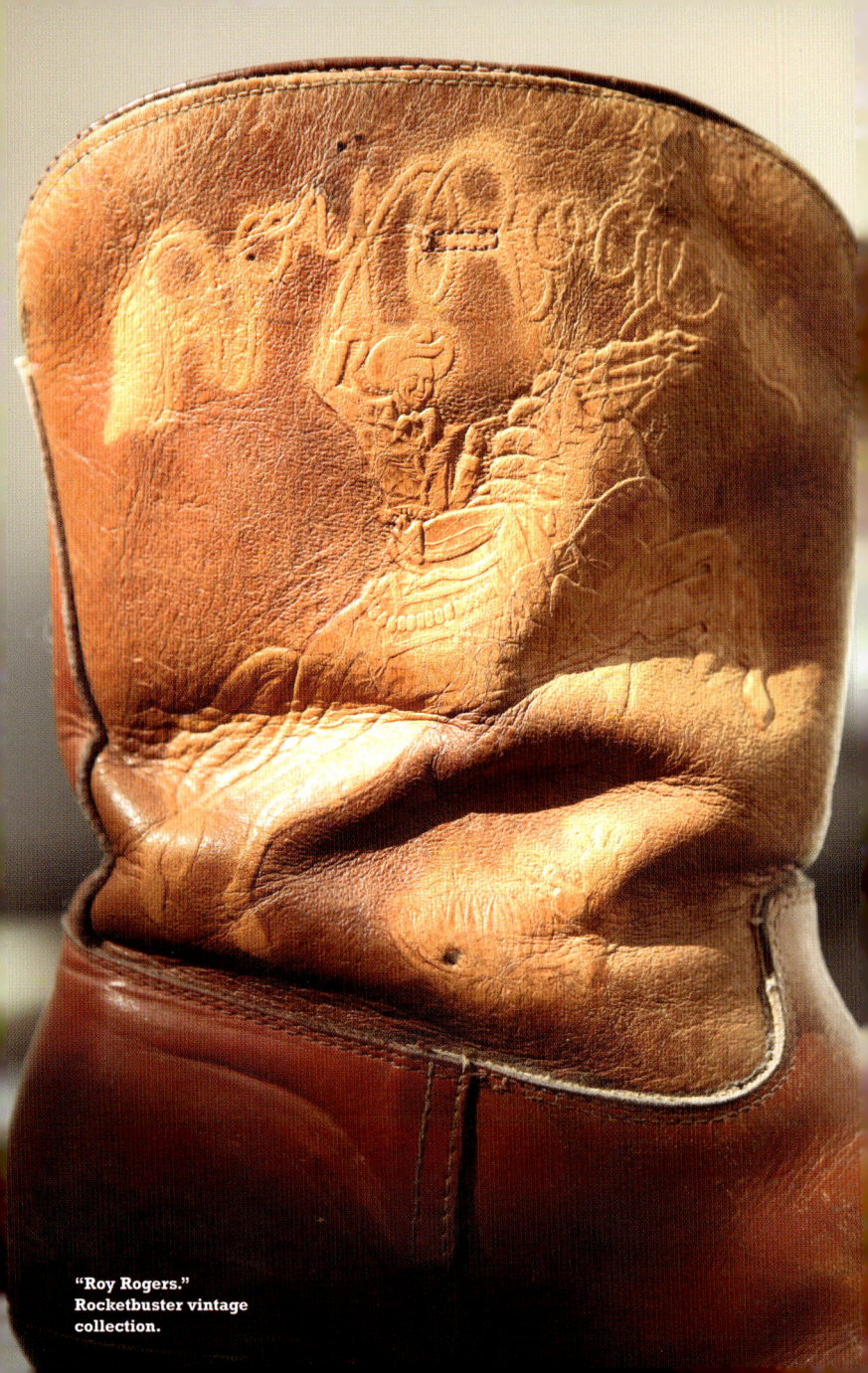

Lattice. Made by Melody Dawkins and Deana McGuffin, Melody's Custom Boots and McGuffin Custom Boots.

Floral scroll. This unique design is symmetrical at the side seam but not the front. Made by McGuffin Custom Boots.

Texas boot pulls. Made by Duck Menzies Bootmaker; courtesy of Wayne Duncan.

"Cactus Shorty."
Made by
Rocketbuster Boots.

"New Mexico" (toe detail). Made by Rocketbuster Boots.

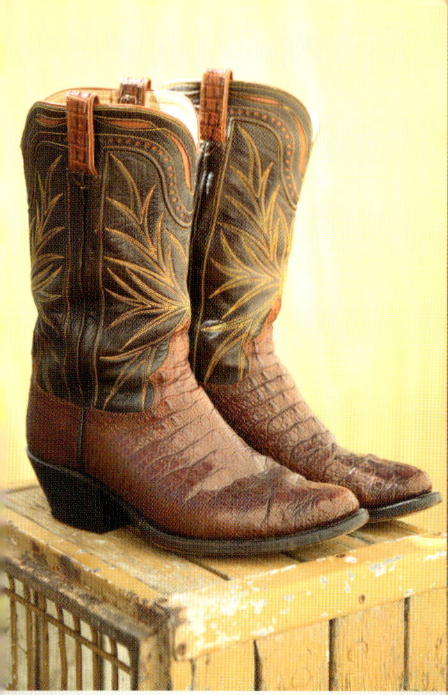

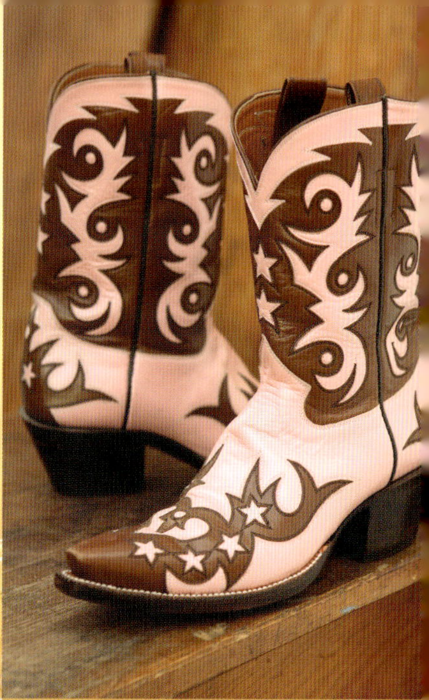

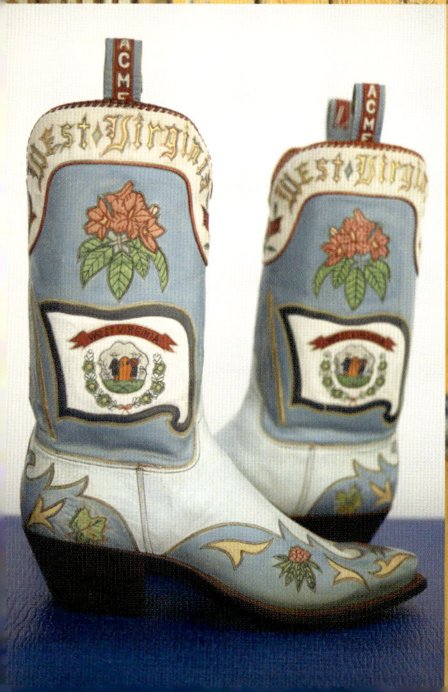
ACME
West Virginia
ACME
West Virgi

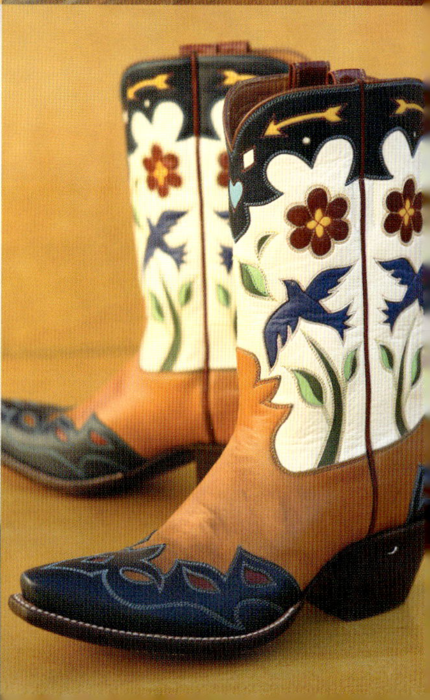

THIS PAGE
top left: Yellow diamond stitched top; courtesy of Mike Hathorn. *top right:* "Happy Trails." Made by Rocketbuster Boots. *bottom right:* Cross. Made by Tres Outlaws.
OPPOSITE PAGE
top left: Hornback lizard. Made by Jesse Bogle; courtesy of David Fox. *top right:* "Raindance." Made by Rocketbuster Boots. *bottom right:* "Little Bird." Made by Rocketbuster Boots. *bottom left:* West Virginia state boot. Made by Lucchese Boot Company circa 1951.

First published in the United States of America in 2007
by UNIVERSE PUBLISHING
A Division of Rizzoli International Publications, Inc.
300 Park Avenue South
New York, NY 10010
www.rizzoliusa.com

Text © 2007 Jennifer June
Photographs © 2007 Marty Snortum, except for those on pp. 35, 41, 268, 284, 303.
See their captions for information.

All rights reserved. No part of this publication may be reproduced,
stored in a retrieval system, or transmitted in any form or by any means,
electronic, mechanical, photocopying, recording, or otherwise,
without prior consent of the publishers.

2007 2008 2009 2010 2011 / 10 9 8 7 6 5 4 3 2 1
Distributed in the U.S. trade by Random House, New York
Printed in China

ISBN-10: 0-7893-1537-8
ISBN-13: 978-0-7893-1537-3

Library of Congress Catalog Control Number: 2006934935

PAGE 1 "Tularosa Star." Made by Rocketbuster Boots.
PAGE 2 Conchos. Made by Wheeler Boot Company.

For my pal Tyler

Your book changed my life into the adventure

it was always meant to be.

State seal. Made by Tres Outlaws.

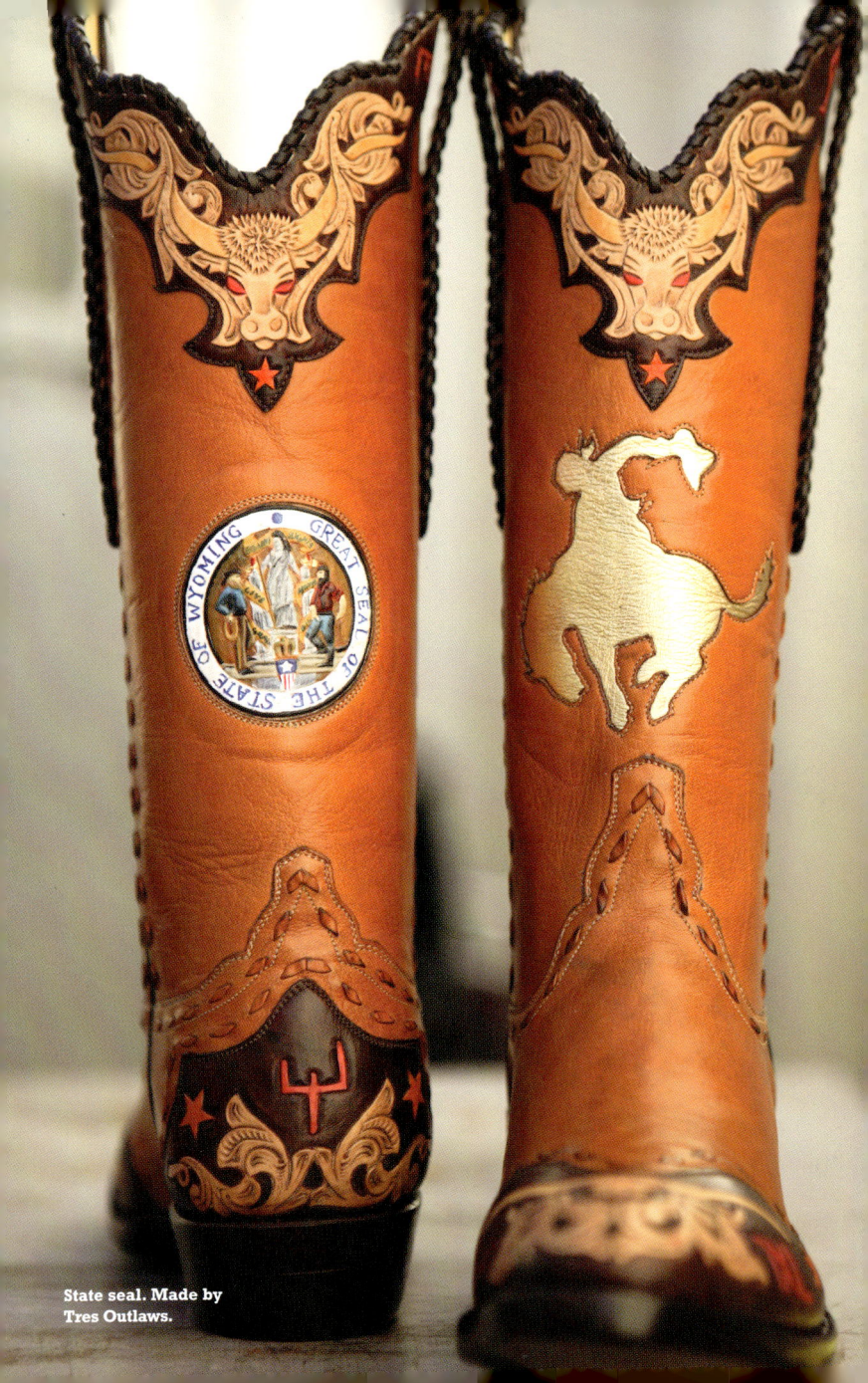

CONTENTS

16	Foreword	311	Glossary
19	Introduction	316	Resources
29	A Brief History	324	Suggested Reading
55	Fancy Boot Tops	327	Acknowledgments
85	Motif and Metaphor		
263	Vintage Cowboy Boots		
275	Sole Searchin': Building a Boot		
309	Final Stitches		

FOREWORD

I doubt that my fascination with the texture, shape, and detail of my first pair of cowboy boots that I excitedly clomped around in at three and four years old throughout the house, the yard, and in the Wild West of my imagination could have foreshadowed the impact that wearing and being associated with cowboy boots, both in motion and at times stoically still, on stage, in photos, and in films would have on my life. But I do recall, even in those early moments of contact with what is arguably the most identifiable element of American fashion iconography (second perhaps only to the cowboy hat), that I viewed cowboy boots as something magically fantastic. Even in the far-flung reaches of the Ohio Valley at the edge of Appalachia where I grew up, I was infatuated by the mystique, myth, and flashy swagger that surrounded the cowboy accoutrements of twin holster gun belts, bandana neckerchiefs, fringe shirts and jackets, fancy spurs, and, of course, the elaborately tooled, stitched, and filigreed cowboy boots that stampeded in a cosmic swirl of trail dust across the screens of late 1950s television. Ironically, the single greatest purveyor of the cowboy culture and mythology that indelibly stamped itself onto the imaginations of countless millions of living-room-romping buckaroos was a quintessential western TV hero who was born in that same Ohio Valley, in the river town of Portsmouth, with the name Leonard Slye. Known to his television legions forevermore as the singing cowboy Roy Rogers, he had been plucked from obscurity in the 1940s from the western movie band *The Sons of The Pioneers*, and, along with the blitzkrieg of cowboy shows that invaded primetime television in the late 1950s through the mid-1960s, he caused an entire generation of young guitar slingers—among them Foghat, The James Gang, ZZ Top, and ultimately myself—to want to strap on a pair of twin holsters, a hat, fancy shirt, suit, and, of course, cowboy boots, and ride the whirlwind of our dreams out of obscure realms and regions.

Many years later, numerous video directors would try to capture my boots in the act of swinging, swiveling, sliding, and roaming through their excited, involuntary reaction to the music I was performing. Their hit-and-miss attempts motivated me to direct my own videos. I had all those childhood images and memories of movie, television, and rock 'n' roll cowboys' heels, spurs, and boots, moving and settling in a very certain and specific way that I wanted and needed to paint with my own hand.

The cowboy boot will be forever linked to feats of daring and chivalry. The legendary leggings of the twelfth-century conquering-Mongol herder-warriors in Asia Minor. The dashingly elegant knee-high cavalry boots of nineteenth-century dragoons in England's romantically doomed charging Light Brigade in the Crimean Wars. The boots ridden to historic glory from the late eighteen hundreds into the twenty-first century by the likes of such disparate bands of New World equestrian marauders as the outlaw James gang, the avenging Texas Rangers, Pancho Villa's guerrilla vaqueros pursued by General "Black Jack" Pershing's U.S. cavalry, and Peter Fonda's fatalistic biker savoir faire as Captain America in *Easy Rider*. They all belonged to a brotherhood of common alliance (albeit at times begrudgingly) based on respect and reverence for each other, and they all shared the use and continued development of this tool of propulsion and symbol of power—the cowboy boot.

With its rakishly distinctive form—undershot riding heel and subtly or severely tapered toe accompanied by various adornments ranging from the stylishly sly to that which borders on extravagance—the classic American cowboy boot appears to possess a sentient vanity all of its own. Its appeal spans a cultural spectrum that includes William F. Buckley and Jerry Lee Lewis, and anyone who has ever come into contact with this icon of the American West knows what it is to lust after a pair. Many of us have been so seduced by the captivating allure of cowboy boots that wearing them is simply an addiction we'll have for life.

Dwight Yoakam, September 2006

In the early 1950s, companies got America to take a fresh look at cowboy boots by using crazy color schemes. Rocketbuster vintage collection.

INTRODUCTION

Worn horse hide. Made by
Dave J. Hutchings' Boots.

Why do people love cowboy boots?
Because they're cool. Because they're loud. Because when you put them on, you can do anything you want to . . . all by yourself.

The frontier is nothing more than the border between the known and the unknown. Each life has its own frontiers, and whenever we're preparing to cross those lines, we reach for our cowboy boots.

Walk like you mean it

Our boots become worn . . . embedded with memories . . . resoled . . . remembered. Cowboy boots are the only footwear that will sit out in plain view even if unworn for years at a time, in a corner or on a shelf. They get buried with loved ones, passed down through generations, or perhaps symbolically left on a fencepost, but never just tossed away.

A pair of cowboy boots gets better with age. Not like sneakers—athletic shoes just run in circles—or "loafers," well, the name says it all.

When you find a cowboy boot in your size, it comes with an odd sense of destiny. A good fit is an omen for great adventure. Find a swell vintage pair and you feel that somehow you are already on your way—that the hardest part of the journey is behind you and the best part is dead ahead.

Face-offs, showdowns, stolen kisses, and narrow escapes

Beauty can be found in a cowboy boot, literally from top to bottom. Boot tops catch and hold our attention. Their colors and patterns are often so bold that they can be admired from clear across the street, dance floor, or corral. We know these stitches—longhorns, butterflies, stars, and moons . . . like words to an old country song or a story we can all recite by heart.

Ah, but wait! There are many boot wearers who would argue that a boot's true beauty lies in its sole, the perfect match of form and function.

In a cowboy boot, you'll find materials used in no other footwear. The rows of wooden pegs that line the shank of a boot are designed to hold a boot together through real-life "hell or high water." Other historical materials, like the 40-penny nail, pounded flat on an anvil to support the wearer's arch, now have modern-day equivalents, yet are still used by many bootmakers in tribute to the traditions of their trade.

Cowboy boots were originally designed for horse and cattle work, and their dependable nature guaranteed their popularity. Nothing breaks quick on a cowboy boot. Laces might suffice for barn work but not for the open range. When you wear out your boots, you see it coming a mile away—a heel slowly wears down, or a sole gradually thins. You might lose a pull strap, but heck, that's what they're there for. Any maker will tell you: if you want to take apart a well-made cowboy boot, "You better get yourself a hacksaw."

Adventure

Most people agree that Hollywood, rather than the stirrup, is responsible for the pointy toe. As the number of actual working cowboys diminished, Hollywood hired actors and filled movie and television screens with larger-than-life renditions. It could be argued that it was then that the cowboy boot's function shifted from fact to fantasy. Like an SUV that's never taken off-road, cowboy boots provide us with the confidence and courage that go well beyond our everyday needs.

Cowboy boots have since walked straight from the choreographed steps of Hollywood to the runways of New York and Paris. They can now be found on the streets of London and for sale secondhand in the stalls of Bangkok's Chatuchak Market.

For most of the cowboy boot's 145-year history, American feet have been dressed in factory-made boots. Texas companies like Tony Lama, Justin, and Lucchese have become household names throughout much of the country. These companies made sure that there was a pair of affordable factory or "shelf" boots within reach of every Roy Rogers, Clint Eastwood, and Dwight Yoakam fan.

Happy trails vs. a clean getaway

Boot factories have always been at the epicenter of fashion's booms and busts. When the widespread boot craze sparked by the 1980 film *Urban Cowboy* faded, it took with it many longstanding trademark factories and America's capacity for mass cowboy-boot production. Today nearly all the labor is done overseas, and factory boot styling has been simplified to cut costs. Leaving us with nothing but round toes and plain stitching.

But for those folks not content with what's sitting on the shelf, for reasons of styling or sizing, there have always been custom boots.

One step at a time

There are 372 steps to building a cowboy boot, including measuring, lastmaking, patternmaking, cutting and assembling pieces, lasting, inseaming, bottoming, and finishing. You can identify some of these steps when you hold a boot in your hand; others are hidden from view by the time a boot is finished and ready to wear. While factories' cost-cutting measures prompt them to speed through, mechanize, and skip all the steps they can, a custom maker's business relies heavily upon his or her careful craftsmanship and ability to attract repeat customers.

There are about 250 custom bootmakers in the United States today—not one of them rich. The number of custom boot shops has doubled in the past ten years, with nearly half of all custom shops outside Texas's borders. Custom bootmaking is by no means a dying art, but it is undergoing an intense period of transition. A few bootmakers like Jack Reed and James Leddy have passed on, and other longtimers like Paul Bond and Dave Little are retiring—handing over the business to their students or families.

These new boot shops differ from the established shops in more than geography. Now women and people of color (primarily Latinos) own and operate their own shops. While these groups of individuals have long traditions in bootmaking, they have often worked anonymously, stitching boot tops and building heels for other (white male) bootmakers.

Custom-made cowboy boots represent the best of both individualism and collaboration. Customers bring a purpose

Hearts and stars are two of the oldest inlay types, mixed here with other inlays derived from typical "flame" stitch patterns. Romero Boots, 1940s; courtesy of Evan Voyles.

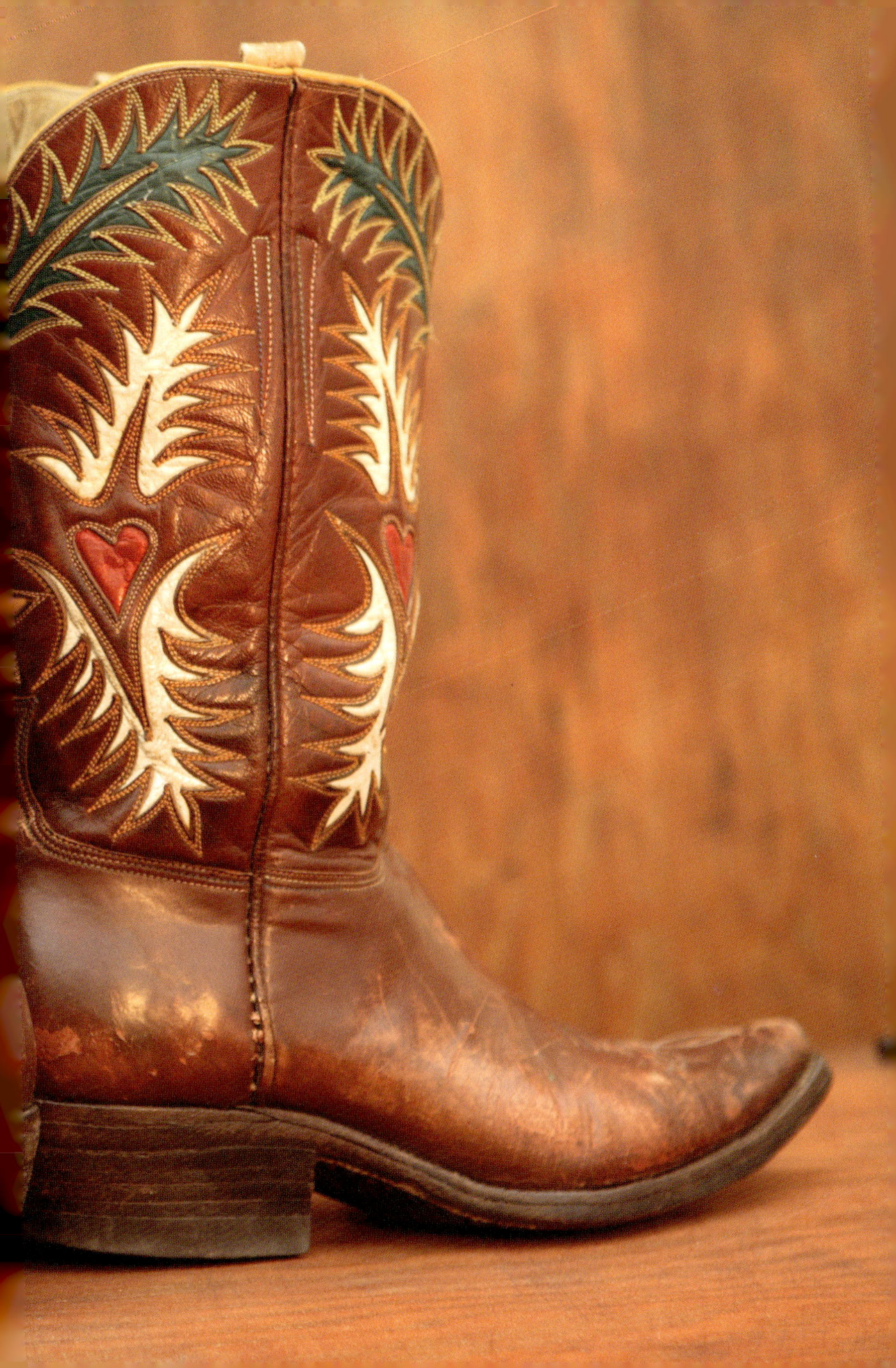

Vintage purple tops; courtesy of D. Alan Calhoun.

and a personality, and bootmakers provide a range of materials, traditions, expertise, and innovation. Custom cowboy boots are a sort of portraiture, full of imagination, meaning, and metaphor.

No boots were specially made for this book. Each pair reflects the independent inspiration and talent of bootmakers and their customers. The boots depicted on these pages have been worn and enjoyed and will remain treasured family heirlooms.

Just as paintings and sculptures tell stories and stir emotions, so do the best cowboy boots.

Walk loud

Stand tall

Step forward.

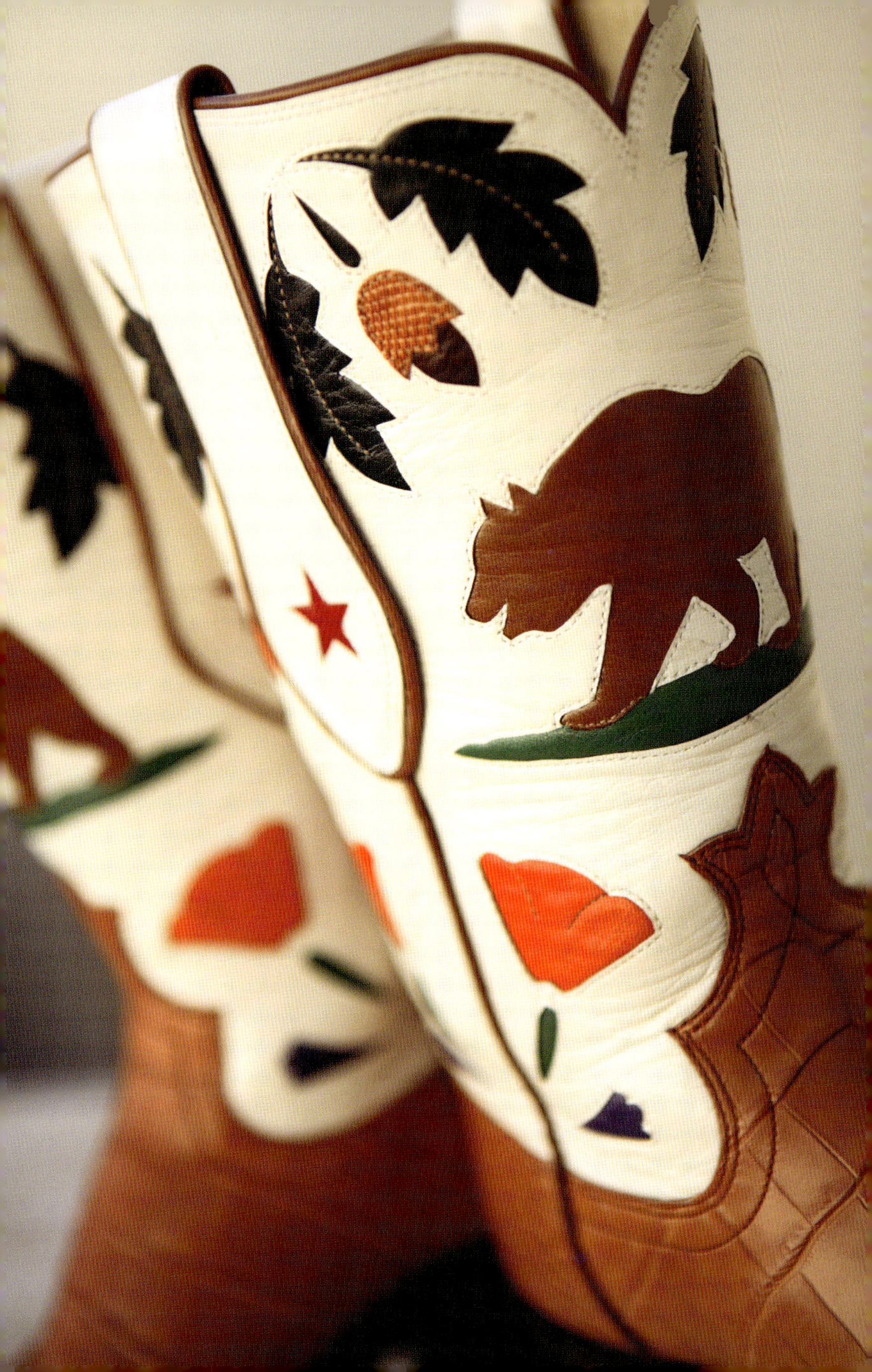

A BRIEF HISTORY

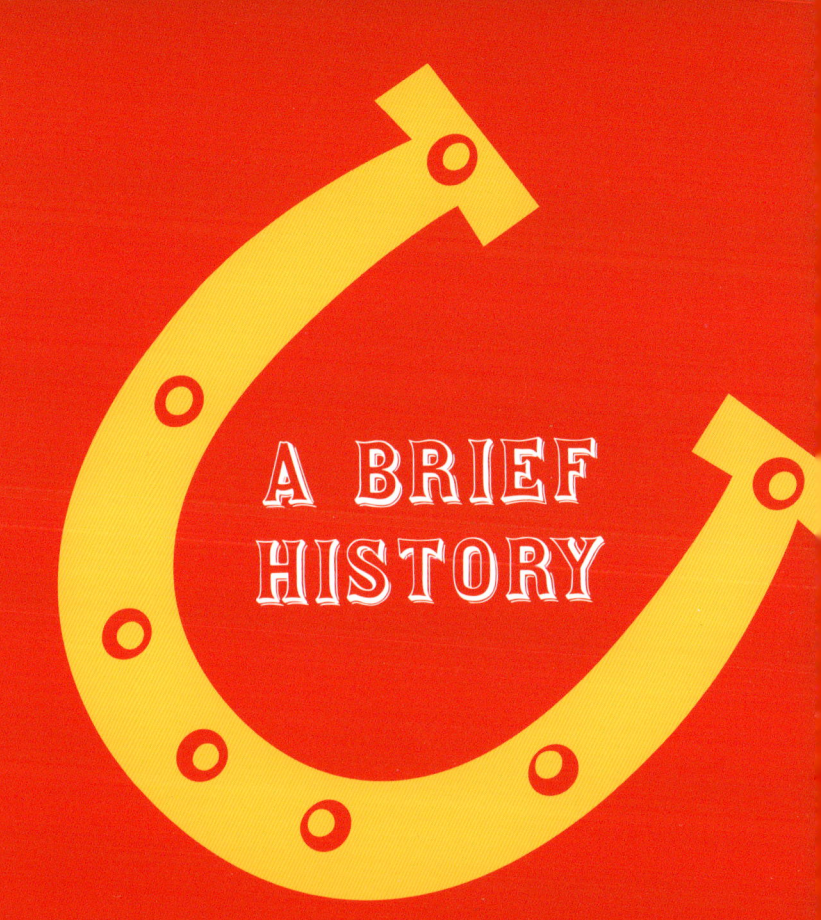

New Mexico state boot.
Made by Lucchese Boot
Company circa 1951.

The history of the cowboy boot is the history of America. Over the past 145 years, you can find evidence of America's economic, political, and social development through a careful look at the cowboy boot.

The story of the cowboy boot begins in the American West.

1860-1880

For as long as men have ridden on horseback, there have been boots, designed to protect against battle and brush. The cowboy lifestyle started in 1867, when Joe McCoy promised forty dollars a head for cattle brought to Abilene, Kansas. This livestock trader and visionary businessman turned the westernmost point of the then-incomplete transcontinental railroad into a booming cow town, as western beef could now be served to eastern diners. Longhorns had roamed the open range since Texas ranchers abandoned their spreads to join the Civil War. Millions of longhorns were "free for the taking," and many others were stolen from Mexican-owned ranches.

Following the Civil War, young men heading west for a new start rode into Texas wearing the same boots in which they had fought the war. Civil War cavalry boots were notorious for their bad construction. Some shoe historians attribute the origins of western bootmaking to the constant repair work required by this repurposed military footwear.

During the 1800s, there was a jumble of boot styles and methods of construction. Popular boots, however, had certain features in common: tall tops to protect feet and legs from the brush, and a heel to help keep feet in the stirrups. The early boot toes were rather round and blunt. Cowboys were known to stand in a water trough and then let the boots dry on their feet as a home remedy for an ill fit. A well-fitting boot helped with horse work by providing cowboys with stability in the stirrups and control of their spurs.

As with almost everything great in America, the cowboy boot is a by-product of ingenuity and immigration. Many of the early bootmakers in the U.S. were German and English

PAGE 28
California boots.
Made by Coe Custom Boots.

immigrants who brought European boot and shoemaking patterns and techniques to the frontier.

In the nineteenth century, fashion trendsetters were often military heroes. The Wellington boot was a style of footwear made popular by Arthur Wellesley, the first Duke of Wellington, who successfully defeated Napoleon at Waterloo in 1815.

What made this Wellington-style boot unique was its four-piece construction: a two-piece top (front and back) and a two-piece foot (vamp and heel counter), similar to today's cowboy boot. Remarkable, too, is the fact that the Wellington boot had a right and left foot; most boots at the time were made using only a straight wooden form, which meant the wearer had to break them in.

Today's well-known boot companies got their start repairing and selling boots to cowboys on cattle drives. C. H. Hyer opened in 1876 in Olathe, Kansas, and H. J. Justin set up shop in 1879 in Spanish Fort, Texas. Like many other western businesses, small boot shops first sprang up along the cattle trails, which were near stockyards and railroad lines. Cities like San Antonio and Fort Worth got a head start in bootmaking, developing an expertise and a legacy that lasts to this day.

1880–1910

By 1880, the cattle drives were over—replaced by barbed wire fences, train tracks, and stockyards. The "golden age of the cowboy" actually lasted less than twenty years.

Myth and fashion took over where history left off. Holly George-Warren, an American entertainment historian, writes, "The marketing myth of the West had begun early in the nineteenth century." First through the written and illustrated travel diaries of adventurers, and then through public exhibitions and performances. William F. Cody was the best-known and most successful western showman. Between 1883 and 1916, *Buffalo Bill Cody's Wild West Show* traveled throughout the United States and Europe. Audiences were introduced to a western cast of cowboys, Indians, frontiersmen, trick riders, and sharpshooters. Performers wore buckskins, boots, wigs,

A Brief History

and war paint—bold western fashions that enthusiastic fans could admire from the bleachers.

It was during this period that rodeos first emerged. Without the cattle roundups once common on the open range, cowboys turned to the rodeo arena to test their skills. Crowds gathered. Boots and chaps were decorated to impress both the judges and those seated in the grandstand.

Around 1885, boot companies like Justin and Hyer began relying on mail-order catalogs to ease communication with customers who had scattered over vast distances. These catalogs and self-measuring kits succeeded in increasing boot sales and name-brand recognition.

> **The invention of chrome leather tanning was a milestone in bootmaking.** Prior to 1890, leather clothing, gear, and boots were made from leather that had been tanned using oils, fats, smoke, or tannins (from plant bark and leaves). Vegetable-tanned leather could take up to a year to produce. Chrome tanning uses a solution of chromium metal that chemically bonds to a protein in the hide—a process that takes minutes instead of years. In addition, chrome-tanned leather is more resistant to heat and longer lasting. And since it is much lighter and more pliable than earlier leather, it allows for colorful leather, finer topstitching, and more comfortable boots.

1910-1929

Silent movie stars like Tom Mix brought boots to the big screen throughout the 1920s and 1930s. The boots were often stitched and inlaid with white flowers, stars, and moons. Film icons of this era typically kept their pants tucked in their boots both on and off the screen, giving decorated cowboy boots a star status all their own.

Soon after their Hollywood debut, cowboy boots appeared in the closets of the general public. First-time customers bought boots from emerging companies such as Tony Lama, Lucchese, and Blucher.

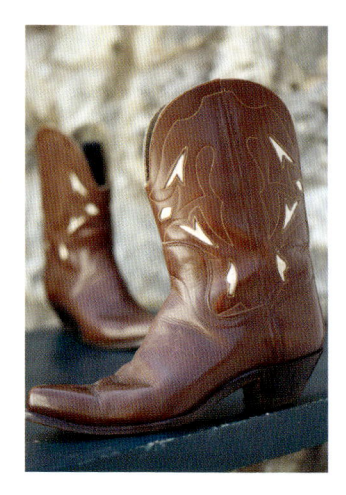

1929-1939

During the mid-1930s, large boot companies like Justin enjoyed increasing sales despite the onset of the Depression. Struggling cattle ranches discovered a new source of income by becoming tourist destinations. These "dude ranches" were not intended for the middle class; they catered directly to wealthy easterners. Boots and western wear were required for ranch activities and made stylish souvenirs to bring back home.

"Dudes" spent their days taking trail rides and having cookouts, not breaking horses or cutting new paths through the brush. Western wear was associated with adventure and fun. Easy on and off short-top boots gained popularity with the wannabe cowboy crowd.

Before the 1930s, women had their boots custom made or they settled for men's boots in small sizes. In 1934, Justin Boots corralled the women's market with its "Western Gypsy," a cowgirl boot with an innovative lightweight sole. It was the first boot built on a last specially made for a woman's foot.

ABOVE Wandering one-row stitch. Made by Kirkendall Boot Company; courtesy of Mark Fletcher. OPPOSITE PAGE Tony Lama promotional postcard circa 1951; collection of Jennifer June.

A Brief History

"EL REY" - *The King of Boots*

$5000.00

Made by the Famous Cowboy
Boot and Shoe Manufacturer

TONY LAMA

EL PASO, TEXAS

Stovepipe top. Courtesy of Phil Noyes.

1939-1945

The cowboy boots of the 1940s reflected the country's economic and political backdrop. The short-top boots shown in the movies became even shorter. "Pee-wee" boots with shorter eight- to ten-inch tops were created to save leather, and boots were sold with simple styling.

Boots made during World War II were either black or brown, due to leather shortages and federal regulations, and bootmakers returned to using stiffer vegetable-tanned leathers. A single row of stitching in matching black or brown was all that was allowed. No fancy boots. For a time, toebugs were outlawed, until Enid Justin, founding owner of Nocona Boots, challenged the statute, asserting that toe stitching strengthened the boot at the point where it flexes—in other words, toebugs were functional and mandatory to a boot's manufacture.

Short tops had sex appeal in the 1940s, showing off a woman's calves at a time when fashion emphasized women's curves.

Since there were no laws against hard work, Justin Boots began selling "made to order" tooled boots for "Dudes and Dudines" in 1941. Justin could turn the existing veg-tan leather into high-priced specialty boot tops. The boot styles had no topstitching but featured elaborate carved scrolls and figurative patterns instead. It was a smart business move, since "made to order" meant that the boots were paid for before any work began.

1945-1960

During World War II, leather and thread were either rationed or unattainable. The years that followed, 1945 to 1955, saw some of the most flamboyant styles in bootmaking history. Colorful inlays and exotic materials appeared with a vengeance.

Bootmakers sought to distinguish themselves from a postwar wave of mass-produced goods and to show off their artistic skill. After years of conservative styling, inlay was now

Montana state boot (detail).
Made by Lucchese Boot
Company circa 1951.

"Batman." Boots fit for a superhero with bat-silhouette stitching and adult-size pull holes. Maker unknown; courtesy of Gary and Shelly Cunningham.

Missouri state boot.
Made by Lucchese Boot
Company circa 1951.

ABOVE
Rex Allen circa 1950. This photo is unusual. Movie stars and performers are typically photographed trying on boots, not visiting with the bootmaker behind the workbench; collection of Jennifer June.

layered and stitched to excess. Abraham and Zeferino Rios of Mercedes, Texas, used padded inlays, metallic leathers, and woven leather lacing, which gave their boots a layered three-dimensional look that was more sculpted than stitched.

Cowboys Roy Rogers and Gene Autry (and cowgirls like Dale Evans) became role models. The silver screen exaggerated boot designs, helping to identify the good guys and the bad. Short boots called "peewees," with their cloth pulls and box toes, were required footwear for travellin' those happy trails.

Following successful careers in radio and film, Gene Autry and Roy Rogers appeared in their own television shows in 1950 and 1951 respectively. The popularity of TV westerns peaked in 1959, with no less than twenty-four shows on prime time each week. "This meant over fifty million Americans were watching westerns every night of the week," according to Michael Marsden and Jack Nachbar in their article "The Modern Popular Western: Radio, Television, Film and Print."

Boot companies like Acme regularly ran ads in *LIFE* and other popular magazines, promoting cowboy boots for the entire family. The 1950s was the first decade in which boot companies dedicated a large portion of their marketing and production budgets to children's boots.

> The "State Boot Series" was a historic project running from 1949 to 1951. Lucchese built a pair of cowboy boots with flags, capitol buildings, flowers, and wildlife to commemorate each U.S. state. Although designed and built by Lucchese, the series was commissioned by Acme Boots and the company's name appears inlayed on each boot pull. After years of touring and display at promotion events, only twenty-two of the original forty-eight pairs are known to exist; the others were stolen or lost to imprecise record-keeping.

Stars and stripes. Made by Cowboy Boots by George.

One-hundred-year commemorative boots. Made by Lucchese Boot Company in 1983; courtesy of Lucchese Boot Company.

1960-1980

The "outlaw" period turned to westerns full of mud, blood, and unshaven heroes. Roach-killer toes and sharp stitching become the main decoration of the almost universally black and brown boots worn by the everyday antihero and rebel. Interest in film and TV westerns began to wane, the likely product of widespread consumer fatigue.

By 1960, rising labor costs and a retail market saturated with western wear and memorabilia led to slumping sales and plainer styles. Discount chain stores forced boot and western wear companies to deliver low wholesale prices.

A burst of color splashed onto cowboy boots as America commemorated its bicentennial in 1976.

1980-1990

The "Urban Cowboy" era (named for the movie starring John Travolta) triggered a stampede back to western wear. Boot companies ramped up production of boots worn mostly on city sidewalks and dance floors. Light-colored leathers, wingtips, and buck stitching got noticed in dimly lit honky-tonks, and rounded toes were forgiving when worn by inexperienced dance partners.

Despite a troubling economic recession, boot sales nearly doubled in 1980. The novelty of exotic hides like python, ostrich, and anteater inspired wearers to buy multiple pairs.

Sharon DeLano's *Texas Boots*, published in 1981, profiled many fine custom cowboy bootmakers while teaching the country about the craft of custom bootmaking.

After the "Urban Cowboy" boom came the bust, taking boot manufacturers by surprise. Demand dropped sharply in 1982, leaving retailers stuck with fashion boots with a short shelf life. Boot manufacturers had also overreacted to the demand, and they found themselves locked into long-range contracts for short-term, trendy exotic skins. In 1983 U.S. plants began to close; this continued throughout the 1990s.

A Brief History

Patchwork. Made by Justin Boots.

Che Guevara. Made by Luis Jovel.

1990–2000

A return to custom bootmaking. The downsizing and closing of a number of factories meant fewer choices of styles and colors on store shelves. America turned to custom makers and vintage boots for fashion flare.

Justin Brands acquired the Tony Lama company in 1990.

In 1992, following in the literary footsteps of DeLano's *Texas Boots*, Tyler Beard and Jim Arndt wrote *The Cowboy Boot Book*, which profiled bootmakers, collectors, and western stores throughout the Southwest. The book stirred new interest in the art of custom bootmaking. Many used the book as a treasure map to find talented bootmakers in remote locations. It also inspired many men and women to pick up the trade themselves.

With the line-dancing craze in the early 1990s, cowboy boots once again broke into mainstream fashion. Line dancing was the perfect solution to traditionally imperfect girl-boy ratios at most dance clubs. People filled the dance floor and left any unwilling partners sitting at the bar. No girls' night out was complete without a pair of western boots for the "stomps" included in many routines. Ill-fitting "Saturday Night Boots" gave cowboy boots a bad rap, spurring many makers to experiment with new materials and to create high-tech comfort soles still on the market today.

Double-headed eagles. Made by Riff Raff Leatherworks; courtesy of Lemmy Kilmister of the band Motörhead.

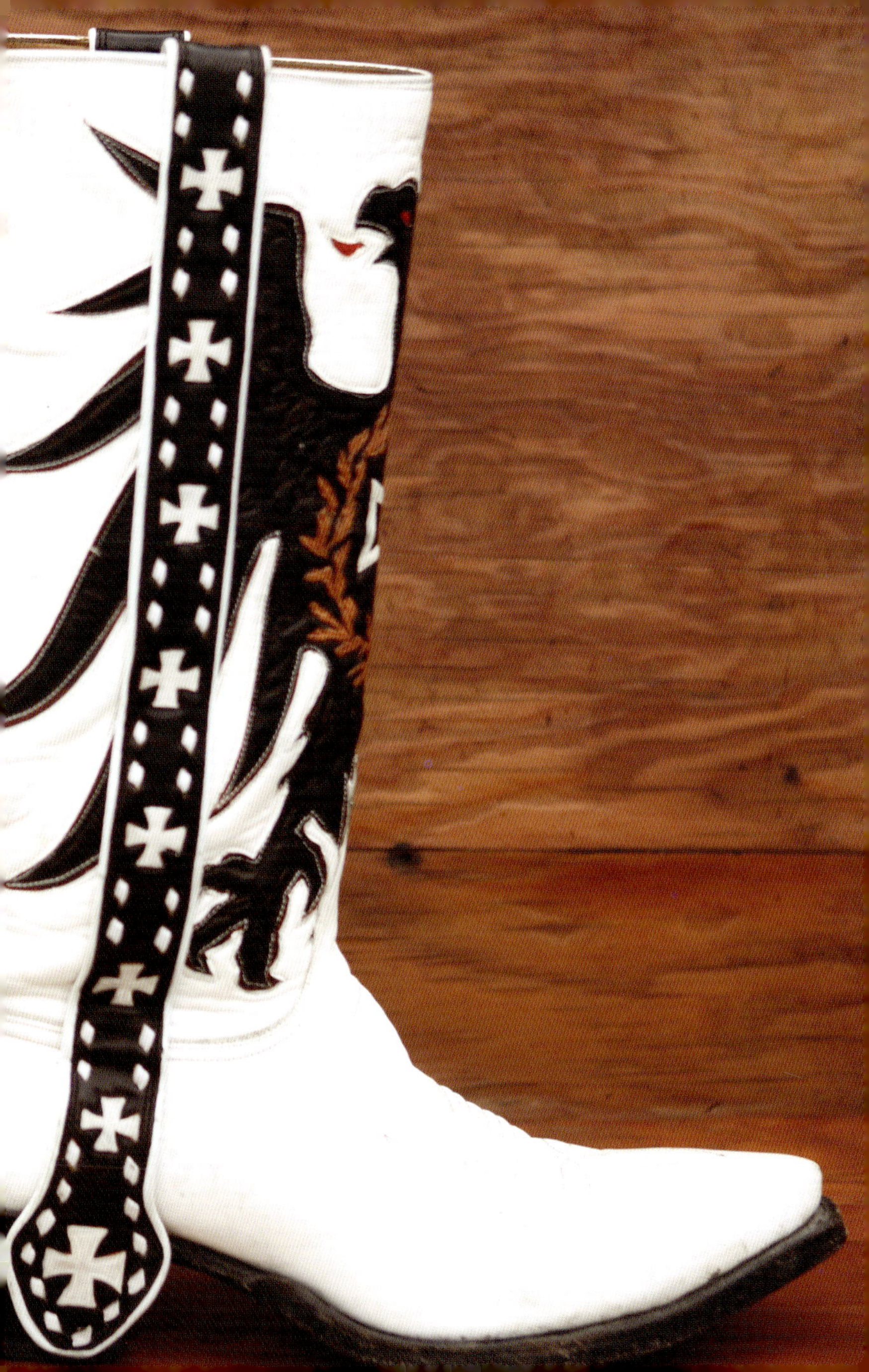

Inspired by vintage Japanese jewelry boxes. Made by Luis Jovel; courtesy of Carolyn Soto.

2000-Today

Retro styles have been reinvented by custom bootmakers who mix traditional boot designs with new, unusual materials and colors. At last, a rebellion against the round toe. What's popular in the new millennium is anything you can't find on the shelf: a plain navy boot for some; hula girls and tiki boots for others.

The Web has put smaller bootmakers on an even footing with large manufacturers by allowing them to showcase their work through homegrown Web sites and to attract customers from around the globe. In a sense, the Internet is a timely upgrade to bootmaking's long tradition of mail-order catalogs.

Today, much of the manufacturing of cowboy boots is following widespread trends of globalization. Nearly 80 percent of Justin boots are made overseas, either in China or India. Mexico's boot and shoe industry lost seven thousand jobs in 2002, in part because of competition from Asia.

The issue of outsourcing cowboy boots is a touchy subject for many reasons. The cowboy boot originated in the American West during a period of optimism and economic expansion, and some consumers regard an imported cowboy boot as somehow inauthentic. Also, many folks still mourn the loss of Texas jobs that existed along the border, in such cities as El Paso and in towns like Nocona—cities with century-long histories of bootmaking. Today's factory-made brands like to boast that the boots are made in "Old Mexico," a term that carries more romance and cachet than Asia.

Current cowboy boot trends offer something for everyone. The "countrypolitan" styles suggest a return to western glamour with high fashion, pointed toes, and even stiletto heels, while the "new" distressed boots represent a rejection of luxury. Lucchese offers styles in which the boots are abraded or "hand worn" to create a rebellious, scratched, and scuffed look.

Steven Weil of Rockmount Ranch Wear points out parallels between the Great Depression and today. "In the 1930s, people sought relief and happiness through their identity with the West, its heroes and its fashion . . . The resurgence of retro western is perhaps a buoyant response to the turmoil of recession and 9/11."

The Future . . .

Cowboy boots will no longer be called "western wear"—instead, they will simply be considered a well-worn foundation of American fashion. Already, today's most fashion-forward styles look as though they were made not from measurements but from memory. With elongated toes and exaggerated toe-bugs, cowboy boots are destined to be reinterpreted along with contemporary fashion trends and the ever-evolving myth of the American West.

Acid-wash horse-hide tops with elephant vamps. You can identify elephant hide by remembering that the leather's grain resembles the folds and creases in the palm of your hand. Made by Tres Outlaws.

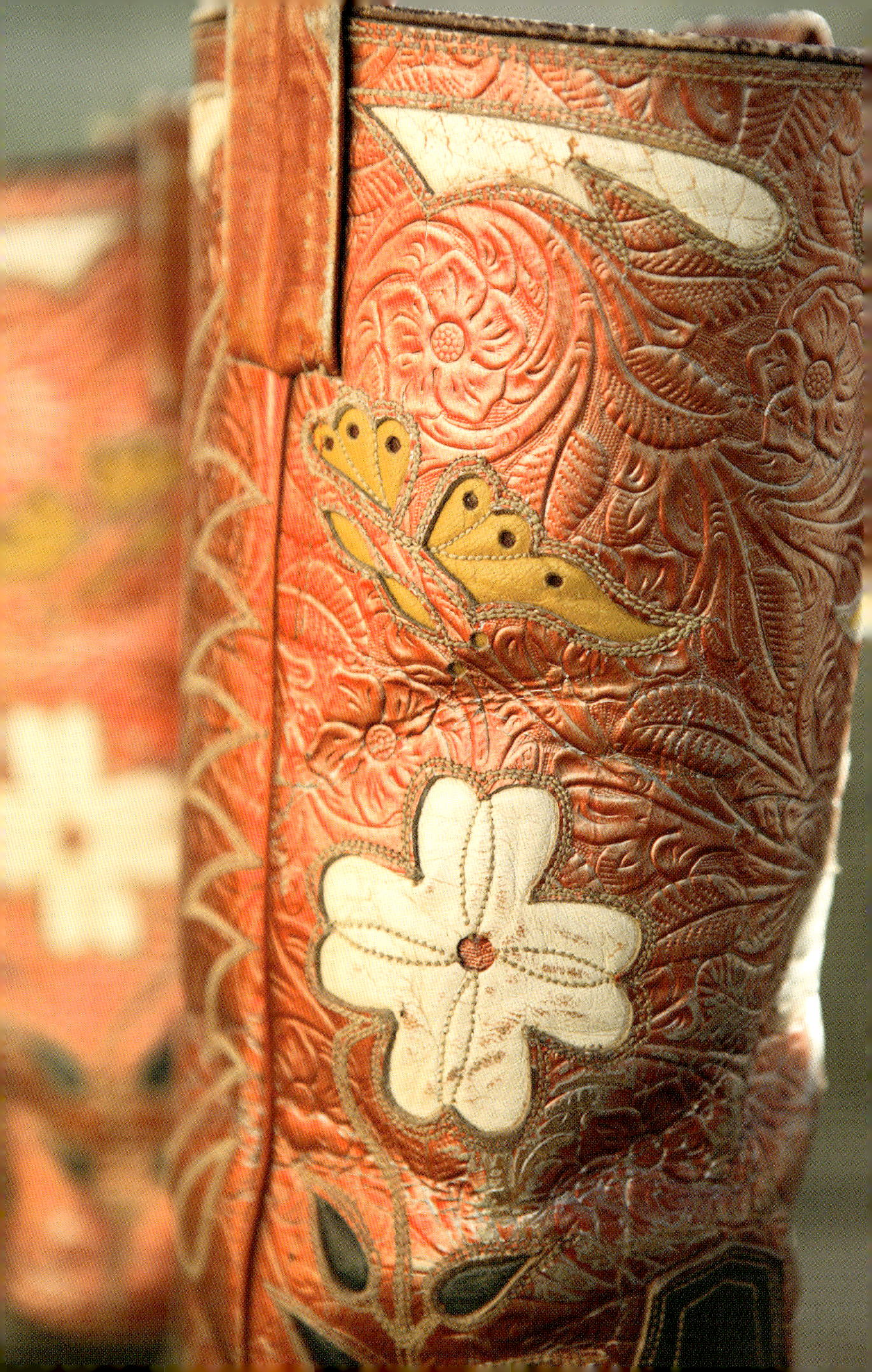

FANCY BOOT TOPS

Black French calf boot with 1937-stitch pattern. Made by Gjelstein Custom Cowboy Boots; courtesy of Abbie Miller.

The decorated cowboy boot has its basis in function, not frivolity. Early boots had a single row or more of stitching to keep the tall tops from sagging. Stitching provides both strength and beauty to a boot top.

Cowboy boots are decorated using several techniques: stitching, inlay, overlay, and leather carving (known as "tooling"). Bootmakers tend to build their professional reputation and legacy on one of these talents.

Stitchwork

Although some might think of a stitched boot as plain, stitching has an element of movement that is rarely seen in inlaid boots. The best stitch patterns can fill the space of a boot top and lead the eye along the pattern's curves and points almost indefinitely. Stitch patterns can be as beautiful and expressive as fancy inlay.

Top stitching on a custom boot is done using a single-needle sewing machine, one row at a time. The bootmaker guides the leather through the machine and lines up the rows right next to each other, about $1/32$ of an inch apart. It's hard work and can take years of practice to perfect.

Traditionally, work boots had one to three rows of stitching, far fewer then dress boots. A pair of Hyer boots, on display at the National Cowboy & Western Heritage Museum in Oklahoma City, Oklahoma, once belonged to rodeo rider Florence Hughes Randolph and features no less than fifteen rows of white stitching.

Some stitch patterns were invented long ago and have been adapted over the years. Other patterns may have been doodled just yesterday while a bootmaker was talking on the phone.

Two bootmakers renowned for their distinctive stitch patterns are Willie Lusk and Ray Jones. It is joked that Ray Jones is well known for his stitch patterns because he gave customers only two to choose from. Willie Lusk is credited with the "inverted flame stitch," a design admired and adapted by bootmakers today.

PAGE 54
Machine-embossed floral. Rocketbuster vintage collection.

Enid Justin, the late Nocona Boots founding owner, admitted that she drew inspiration for her early stitch patterns from unusual sources. For instance, a handful of her early patterns resembled the curves and scrolls in her brocade couch. While at a funeral for a local banker, she dreamed up a stitch pattern based on the wrinkles on the neck of an old man sitting in front of her. In her autobiography, Miss Enid remarked that her sketch took nearly the entire service to complete, because each time the man bowed his head to pray, the wrinkles in his neck would temporarily disappear.

Boot stitching frequently provides clues to its maker ... if you know where to look. Many times there is a short row or two of stitching on the side, near the side seam and below the wearer's ankle. This row of stitches may take a sharp turn, zigzag, or seem to loop unnecessarily. These stitches are not initials, nor do they hold a label, but they are a maker's mark.

Clues to a boot's maker can also be found in the "toebug" or "toe flower." Bootmakers will often choose one design and stick with it throughout their career. It acts as a signature and identifies the boot even without the wearer having to lift a cuff.

Inlay and Overlay Designs

Bold colors and shapes on cowboy boots are typically the results of overlaid and inlaid leathers. Layers of colorful leather are either stitched on top of a boot top (overlay) or underneath (inlay), with the shapes cut out of the boot top so the colored inlay shows through. The edges of the inlay and overlay are thinned with a sharp knife so that the seams around the decorative work lie flat. Inlay can be simple or ornate, with designs made up of dozens of small pieces of leather.

When space allows, many of the best bootmakers will put two rows of stitching around an inlay or overlay pattern. It requires more than twice the skill to follow the tight curves and cutouts a second time, with smooth rows of stitching sewn side-by-side.

Large boot factories have computerized stitching machines that can stitch a "ten row" boot top in seconds.

Fancy Boot Tops

The small loop of blue stitches found near the side seam identifies the boot's maker, Duck Menzies; courtesy of James Willett.

The visual balance on this boot is achieved by increasing the rows of stitching. Five rows on the foot, ten rows on the tops, and fifteen near the collar. Original Lucchese Boot Company design remade by Glenderson Daly, SAS Shoemakers; courtesy of John Tongate.

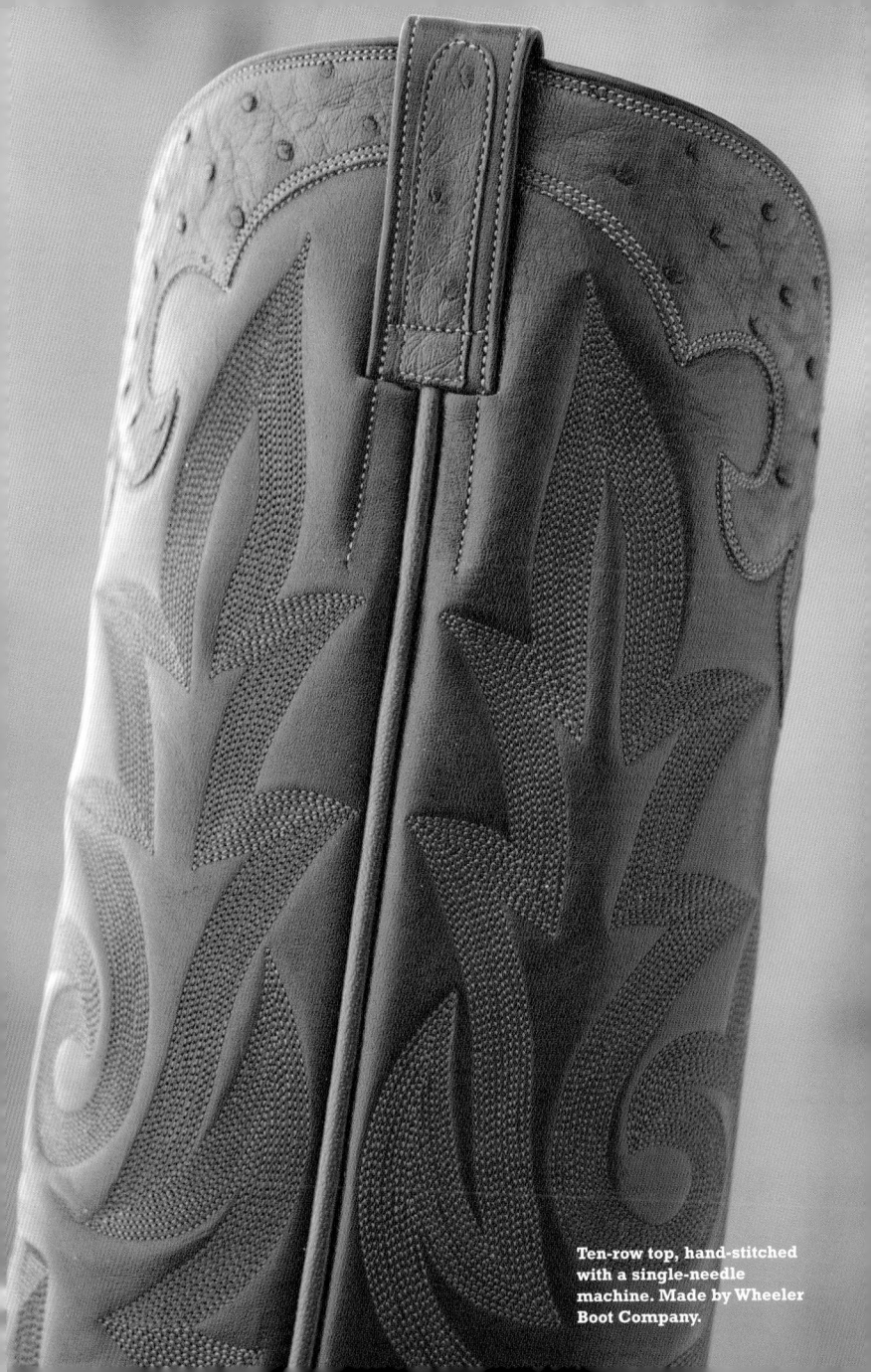

Ten-row top, hand-stitched with a single-needle machine. Made by Wheeler Boot Company.

Inverted flame stitch. Made by James Leddy Boot Company; courtesy of John Tongate.

Diamond stitch. Made by Richard Cook Custom Boots; courtesy of James Willett.

Lions. Made by Dew's
Custom Handmade Boots

Overlay and inlay are commonly used together. For instance, a brown boot might have a white overlay at the top of the boot, forming a "collar," and the collar might have an inlay of, say, a small red heart.

Shapes and colors repeated across a boot top can provide balance and rhythm to a boot design ... almost like the chorus of a song.

Leather Carving

Tooled leather is something many people recognize from the patterns and textures of decorated saddles. Carved flowers, scrolls, and acanthus leaves fill the awkward shapes and forms of a saddle and meld it into a single piece of art.

It is not a far leap from saddle stirrup to boot top. Leather tooling is a favored way to give a true western look to a cowboy boot.

In order to transfer a drawn design onto a boot top, the leather is first dampened and then cut with a sharp blade. Using small hand tools and a rawhide mallet, the tooler stamps around the cuts, giving the leather depth and shape. Accents and details are created with specially shaped stamping tools, such as small decorative circles for the centers of flowers. The finished boot top gets a thin coat of stain to darken the shadows, emphasize the designs, and seal the leather.

Leather carvers can put in as many as three hundred hours on a single pair of boots. New patterns are drawn for nearly every pair. Even classic tooling designs must be redrawn in order to correctly fit a customer's boot measurements. The tooler seeks to fill the space and achieve a balanced design. This can be quite a challenge when a customer requests unusual flora or fauna, or epic scenes like the fall of the Alamo.

In the early 1940s, Justin Boots offered a line of hand-tooled made-to-order cowboy boots. These boots were meant to be admired close up, with the lift of a cuff, not from the rodeo grandstands. These boots also provided a practical and artful way to sidestep the wartime rationing of silk (used in thread) and chrome (for leather tanning). Paid for in

Red trim. Made by Janet Stoddard Custom Boots; courtesy of James Willett.

Yellow rose overlay.
Made by Little's Boots.

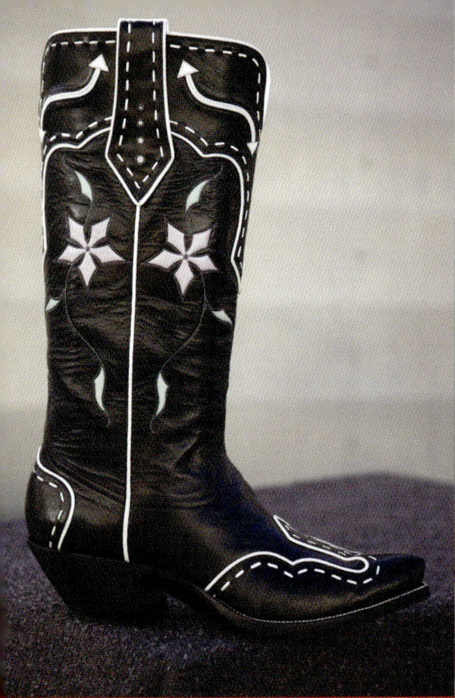
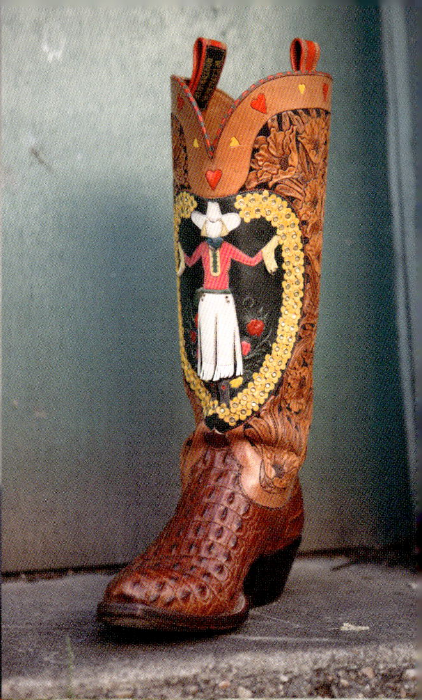
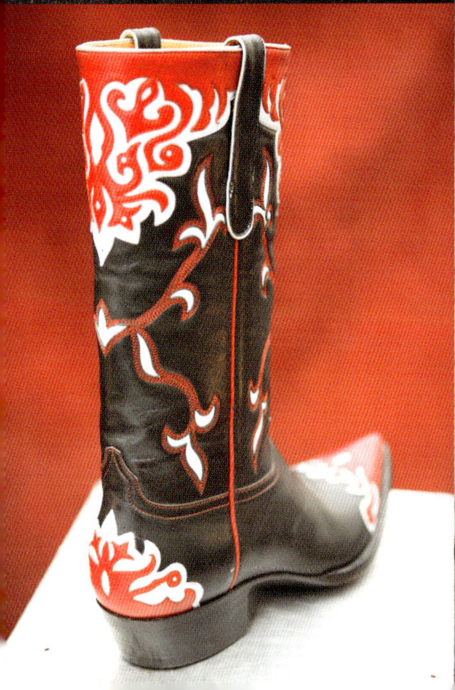
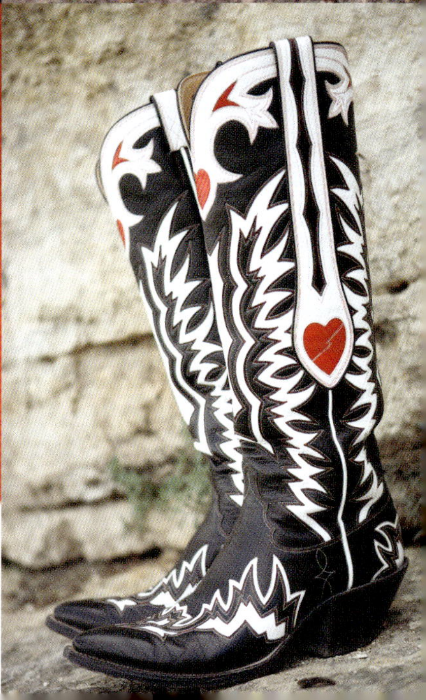

Northwest. Made by Wild Bill's Boots; courtesy of Jeff Borins.

Limited edition boots (only two hundred of this style will be sold). Made by Paul Bond Boot Company.

Abstract inlay. Made by
Custom Boots by Morado;
courtesy of John Tongate.

"Hand-tooled Grape Leaf and Vine." Made by Back at the Ranch.

PAGE 68 *top left:* Western wear. Inspired by western shirts of the 1950s, this boot features a saddle-stitch accent, crooked smile "pockets," and arrow overlays. Made by Sorrell Custom Boots; courtesy of Walker Wells. *top right:* Sweetheart of the rodeo. Design adapted from Jo Mora's 1933 illustration. This image was made famous when The Byrds used it as album cover art. Made by William Shanor; courtesy of Barbara J. Couture. *bottom right:* Tall top inlay. Made by Tex Robin Boots; courtesy of James Willett. *bottom left:* Delicate inlay. Made by Liberty Boot Company.

advance by wealthy easterners, the styles carried names like the "Acorn," the "Saddlemaker," and the "Fandango" (featuring a dramatic flamenco dancer with castanets). Other popular design figures at the time included rodeo riders, bucking broncos, eagles, and of course, stars.

Carved leather is unsuitable for work boots. Since leather carvers cut and stamp their designs into damp leather, the moisture and flexing that comes with heavy use and wear will flatten a design. Even the tooling on vintage boots tends to "soften" with age. Some vintage painted pieces appear to hold their designs better because the paint is better able to resist moisture and the color continues to delineate the edges of the patterns.

By contrast, contemporary toolwork looks strong and deep. Boot collector Jeff Borins attributes this in large part to the quality of leather and tools being used today. Many old-timers used a stiff steel blade rather than the swivel knife that is now widely available.

Many tooled cowboy boots use laced side seams or one-piece "regal" tops in order to protect the tooler's hard work and delicate design details during the construction of the boot. When you make a two-piece top with machine-sewn side seams, the boot is constructed inside out and must then be rolled right-side out before being lasted—potentially erasing much of the tooler's efforts.

Just as there is a difference in the value and prestige of cut crystal versus pressed glass, boot collectors should not confuse embossed leather with tooled leather. On embossed leather, the pattern is stamped with rollers, and the floral or scroll details have soft edges and the repeating pattern continues across the boot leather, paying no mind to seams or edges.

As mentioned by boot expert Tyler Beard in his book *Art of the Boot*, the early 1990s brought a renewed interest in hand-carved and tooled cowboy boots.

Rocketbuster Boots popularized the use of tattoo flash as patterns for leather tooling on short-topped boots. Iconic figures such as hula girls and sailing ships work well on boots despite their obviously non-western themes. A pant leg takes the place of a shirt sleeve, and the natural beige color of the boot leather mimics human skin.

By the late 1990s, clusters of grapes carved onto boot tops started to appear. As symbols of wealth and prosperity, these boots proved popular not only with vineyard owners but also with wine collectors and connoisseurs. Grape clusters lend themselves well to tooling with their trailing vines, scrolling leaves, and small fruit. Some of these boot tops are then hand painted, but grape-themed designs are easy to recognize by their shapes alone.

Leather tooling provides the effect closest to realism and portraiture.

"Time is money."
Benjamin Franklin, American diplomat and inventor

The high-end boot customer knows there's nothing more precious than time. In the past five years, tooling has taken on greater popularity as a sign of luxury, taking the place of exotic skins like crocodile on the vamps of high-priced boots. Cowboy boots are now tooled both top and bottom. Color and depth are being added with the use of filigree, a technique in which the background of a tooled top is cut out. The top is lined with colored leather, often with a shiny reptile hide like lizard to kick back light and color.

Leather-tooler Howard Knight recently tooled an astounding pair for a customer of Axel's in Vail, Colorado. Boasting a selling price of more than sixty thousand dollars, the boots feature a filigree pattern backed by sterling silver.

Although they are closely associated, bootmaking and tooling are separate crafts. Few bootmakers are also experienced leather toolers—the short list includes Carman Allen, Ty Skiver, and Pascal. Some larger boot companies consistently have enough orders that they can employ a leather tooler full time, but most bootmakers develop working relationships with multiple toolers. Among the best known are Knight, Karla Van Horn, Roy Pohja, Shirley Robinson, Carey Blanchard, and the late Bob Dellis.

Fancy Boot Tops

Tooled posey with inlay.
Made by Olsen-Stelzer
Boot Company; courtesy
of D. Alan Calhoun.

"Tularosa Pintado." Made by Rocketbuster Boots.

"Side Saddle." Made by Rocketbuster Boots.

"Autumn." Made by Liberty Boot Company.

Rich texture shown on crocodile boots with hand-tooled overlay. Made by Tres Outlaws.

"She Devil." Made by Rocketbuster Boots.

Exotic Leathers

For maximum impact, an exotic leather should offer novelty and surprise. Bystanders will wonder, point, and eventually ask, "What is it?" Popular with people who want to stand out in a crowd, exotic leathers provide eye-catching patterns and textures not found on everyday cowhide.

In many cultures, wearing the skin of or eating a totemic animal is thought to convey that animal's strengths and characteristics: cunning, speed, and virility, to name a few. In a similar fashion, cowboy boots made with exotic leathers send strong subliminal messages about the wearer's wealth, status, and sexual prowess.

Exotic leathers come from reptiles like alligators, snakes, and lizards; mammals such as anteaters and elephants; and even sea creatures, including eels, stingrays, and sharks.

Because of their expense, glossy shine, and rather delicate nature, exotic leathers are typically best suited to dress boots. Eel and snake skins are thin and prone to rips and tears, even during the boot's manufacture. When worn every day, these boots wind up looking like roadkill.

Shark and elephant skin are two exceptions. Both are thick and sturdy skins, commonly mistaken for bullhide, and they wear well and are sought after for durable work boots.

Exotic skins used to make cowboy boots are subject to federal and state regulations. Much of the alligator skin now comes from domestically farmed animals; however, many of the snakes, lizards, and mammals are still hunted in their native habitats. Although you can still find vintage samples of sea turtle and anteater boots, these animals are now endangered. New boots are no longer being made, and in all but a few circumstances, even selling vintage pairs is illegal.

Optical illusion. The "side seam" on this boot was created by nature, not the bootmaker. Made by Tres Outlaws.

Pangolin (anteater) hide has a distinctive diamond pattern; it is no longer legally imported. Vintage boot made by Little's Boots.

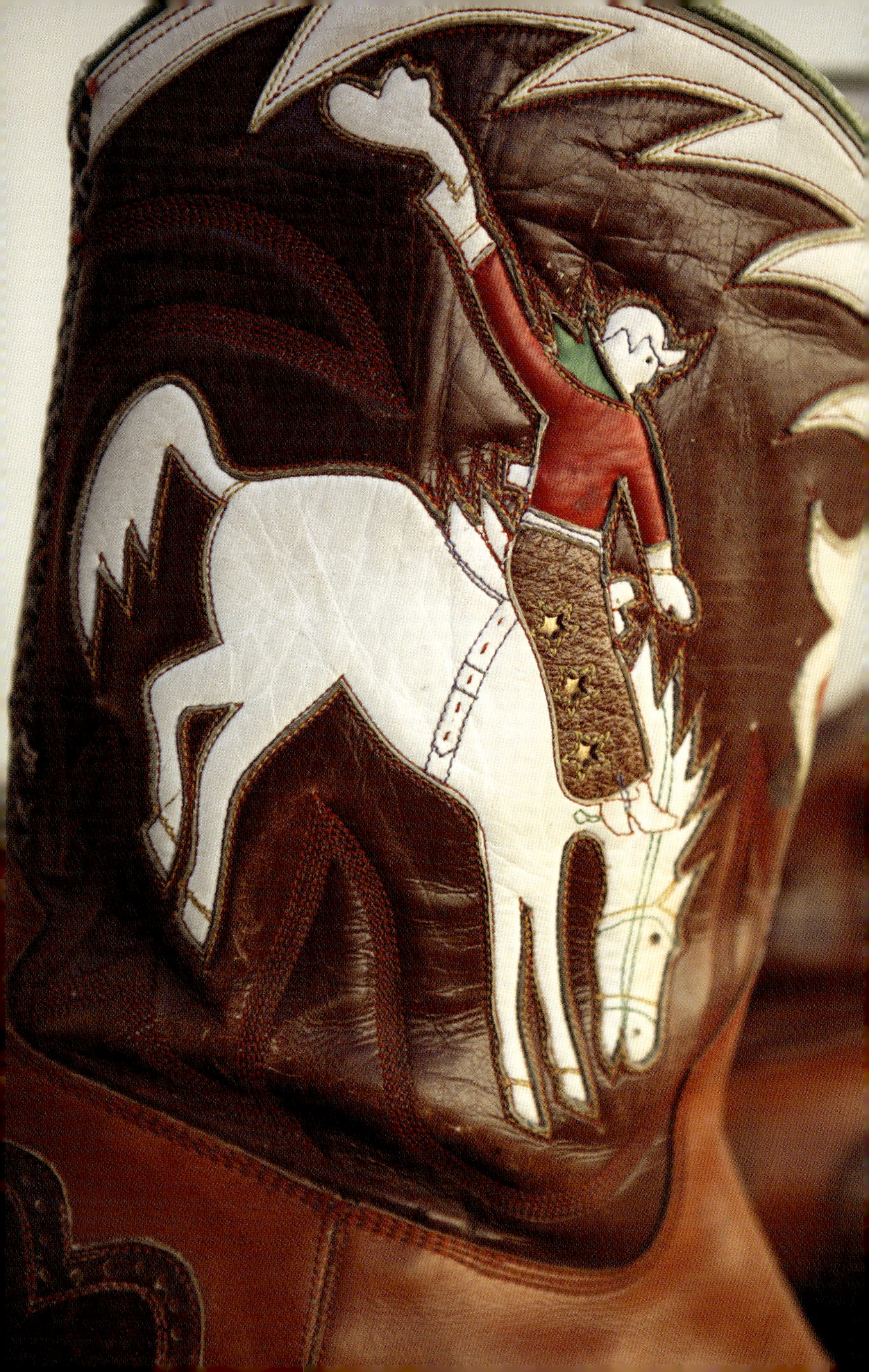

MOTIF AND METAPHOR

Ace. These boots belong to rockabilly star Rosie Flores with trademark rose inlay and blue guitar. Made by Janet Stoddard Custom Boots.

A **boot doesn't get to be called "art" just because its inlay is impressive and its stitches are straight.** It needs to tell a good story. There are many talented bootmakers in America who have mastered their materials and techniques. One can portray nearly anything on a boot—and unfortunately people have.

Images of bass fishing, flamingos, and even the family dog have been stitched into boot tops. And while these boots may showcase a bootmaker's skill, they are rarely as successful as a pair with just the simplest star cutout.

Try this test. Stare at a cowboy boot. If you are swayed by its realism and its stitches' twists and turns, the boot may well be the product of unparalleled craftsmanship. If, however, you look at a boot and find it impossible to concentrate—your mind hopelessly wanders to memories of a road trip, a lover who broke your heart, or a personal dream left unfulfilled—then the boot before you is most likely a work of art.

Messages portrayed on boots change over time . . . trail markers of a larger American story. As time passes, certain symbols lose their meaning while others step up to take their place. One example is the oil derrick, inlaid in gold on Texas-made Nocona Boots throughout the 1940s. They were worn not just by oil tycoons, but by anyone claiming to have "struck it rich." Nowadays the oil derrick is seldom seen on custom boots, having been replaced by exotic hides, corporate logos, or dollar bill imagery.

Not every boot is a biography of its owner. While individuals will be drawn to a particular pair of boots, it is more useful to study the boots for the story they tell about America, about where we've come from and who we aspire to be.

Where barbed wire on a boot once symbolized conquest and prosperity, in an increasingly urbanized America, it has assumed connotations related to escape and the arbitrariness of geographical and ideological boundaries.

PAGE 84
Fancy duds.
Maker unknown;
courtesy of Karen Robinson.

Variations on themes . . . an unusual take on a well-worn symbol. These motifs and metaphors have appeared on thousands of boots. More fascinating than the emergence of dominant themes are their endless variations.

"Hipchick Beatnik/Lariat Gal." Made by Gina C. Guy.

"La Pareja" (the pair). Made by Rocketbuster Boots.

Campfire. Texas Traditions Boots by Lee Miller; courtesy of Joe Guzzardi.

Saguaro. The sueded brown background and simple inlay create a remote landscape. Maker unknown, 1940s.

"Cielo Lindo" (sweet sky).
Made by Liberty Boot
Company.

Flora and Fauna

Stitched into both factory and custom boots, the flora and fauna of the western landscape are portrayed on boots more than any other type of imagery. Butterflies and birds are metaphors for freedom of movement; wild flowers and stars conjure open expanses of land. Snakes and bucking broncos, even chili peppers, suggest danger and adventure. This scenery belongs to an idealized landscape that is "the West" of our imagination. Perhaps as we watch the authentic West becoming more populated and urbanized, our cultural hold on these symbols tightens.

Flowers

Flowers were among the first inlays stitched on a boot top, and they have brought color and beauty to bootmakers' work for nearly a hundred years. One of the most popular Nocona boots has a simple star-shaped posy; this imaginary flower has been reproduced by bootmakers over and over.

Many flowers tend to be very basic in design; factory boots have no patience for fancy inlay. Linked leaf shapes, floating petals; flowers are suggested, but not detailed. Stems and leaves are drawn with erratic stitches, sometimes resembling tumble weeds. It is the simple and "wild" flowers that remain timeless, which in a western landscape can represent "transience of earthly existence as well as the promise of eternal life," according to Briane Turley in his article "Religion as Art: Gravestone Iconography in West Virginia."

The enduring popularity of flowers can be seen as a gesture that pays homage to the here and now. Once upon a time, a cowboy in the West could happen across a flower, knowing he was the only person who would witness its blooming.

There is a special nostalgia stitched into many a flower inlay. With transience often comes a sense of longing for endless, untamed lands . . . and adventure.

Flower patch. Made by Kimmel Boots; courtesy of Bryce Sunderlin.

Small, green lizard-hide inlays add texture and realism to the flowers' cones. Texas Traditions Boots by Lee Miller; courtesy of Joe Guzzardi.

"Calabasas." Made by Liberty Boot Company.

"Cattail Boot." Made by
J. B. Hill Boot Company.

"'60s Cowgirl." Made by Liberty Boot Company.

The cherry blossom branches make good use of this triad boot design. Made by Caboots; courtesy of Priscilla Sanchez.

Stages of bloom.
Texas Traditions
Boots by Lee Miller.

Red flowers and pulls.
Made by Ramirez & Sons
Boot Manufacturing;
courtesy of John Tongate.

Roses

"The rose is the most prominent image in the human brain, as to delicacy, short-livedness, thorniness . . . There is no better allegory for, dare I say it, *life*, than roses."
Robert Hunter, lyricist for the Grateful Dead

Red, yellow, white, pink; the rose's rounded petals and pointed green leaves are easily recognized. Roses have been important artistic symbols for hundreds of years, and they look beautiful on a cowboy boot. While roses are wild and thorny on vintage boots, now they have a more cultivated look, adding luster and refinement to an otherwise ornery piece of footwear. Like the tulip used in lush, deep colors, the rose today calls to mind an image of a tended garden rather than the untamed West.

The well-known song "The Yellow Rose of Texas" tells of a man's love and longing for a woman. A yellow rose on a cowboy boot has since taken on the broader symbolism of "home."

On men's boots, roses are often well-kept secrets. Even when a man is asked to lift his cuff, a rose inlaid near the pull strap is seldom revealed.

Bootmakers use many different techniques to capture the beauty and significance of a rose. A rose is frequently inlaid with cotton stuffing behind it to invoke a fuller bloom. Countless petals can be overlaid and hand-stitched, making each flower unique.

Texas bootmaker Charlie Dunn is remembered for his "pinched" roses. Mysteriously molded, the finished roses have a three-dimensional depth rarely achieved with overlay. The secret to making pinched roses is a Texas tradition that was handed down to bootmaker Lee Miller before Charlie's death.

Roses are also a popular pattern with leather toolers. Roses are quickly recognized no matter how they are oriented. A bootmaker or carver can fill a boot top with balanced color and design by tilting or leaning the rose's scroll-like leaves and petals. While men tend to prefer a four-petal wild rose, women's boots are embellished with more familiar garden-grown varieties. Often the roses are inked or stained rather than painted, and the soft colors lend the work a rather dreamy appearance.

By using roses in various stages of bloom, a bootmaker can create an artistic design and a subtle allegory of an individual life. Roses in full bloom can imply beauty, luxury, or even sexuality, depending on their owner. Rosebuds are delicate and full of potential, and thorns can be bold and menacing . . . or suspiciously absent.

Butterflies

No doubt about it, butterflies are God's gift to bootmakers: bright, colorful, and absolutely symmetrical. But while color and convenience might explain the bootmaker's fondness for this insect, why do they appeal to the rest of us?

Like so many winged western critters, butterflies invoke the feeling of wide-open spaces and freedom of movement. But there's more . . .

Butterflies, like the American West, are enduring symbols of personal transformation . . . of metamorphosis.

Custom-bootmaker John Weinkauf is well known for his butterfly inlays: one large butterfly on the front of each boot, with multicolored wings wrapping around to the side seams. When asked about his signature stitch, he responds that people just keep asking for them over and over again. While bootmaker Paul Bond notes that men nearly always leave off the flowers, even the roughest, toughest cowboys have a soft spot for butterflies, which traditionally were depicted in equal numbers on men's and women's boots.

Cowboy boots featuring butterflies have been around since the 1920s, appearing first on custom boots, then on factory boots such as Acme and Texas Boots.

Because of the curve of their wings and their real-life flight patterns, butterflies can look "natural" when positioned

"Yellow Rose." Made by Rocketbuster Boots.

A sorrowful variation on the art of the 1600s, in which roses strewn at one's feet often symbolized a short life. Worn by Teresa Beard; courtesy of Tyler Beard. Made by Kimmel Boots.

The high heel and lacing on this boot give it the femininity of a silk stocking. Designed by Corinne Joy Brown; made by Tres Outlaws.

Red and white roses. The top is made of hair-on cowhide. Made by Charlie Dunn, Texas Traditions; courtesy of Donald Counts.

THIS PAGE
top left: Butterfly, 1950s. A design cutout more typical of a 1930s boot, with rarely seen "cactus flower" inlays. Note the distinctive black-leather lining. Made by Economy Boot Shop; courtesy of Evan Voyles. *top right:* Nothing girlie about these vintage butterfly boots. Made by Stewart Romero; courtesy of Mark Fletcher.
OPPOSITE PAGE
top left: Butterflies on brown. Made by Sorrell Custom Boots. *top right:* Spotted wings. Variegated thread around the butterfly gives it a flutter. Made by Stallion Boot Company. *bottom left:* "Vintage Butterfly." Made by Liberty Boot Company. *bottom right:* Sawtooth collar. Made by Blucher Custom Boots; courtesy of Jesus Lujan.

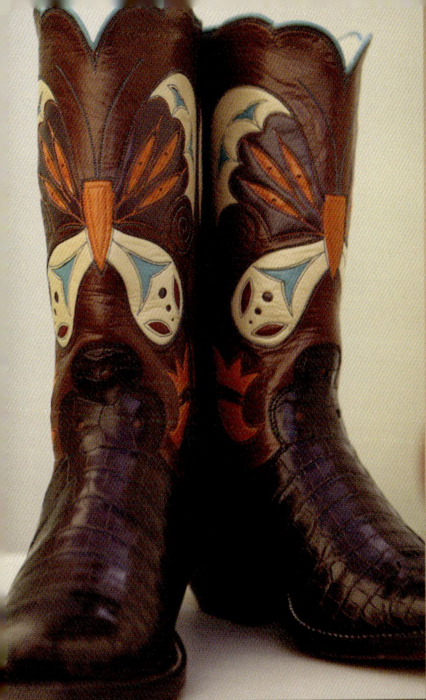
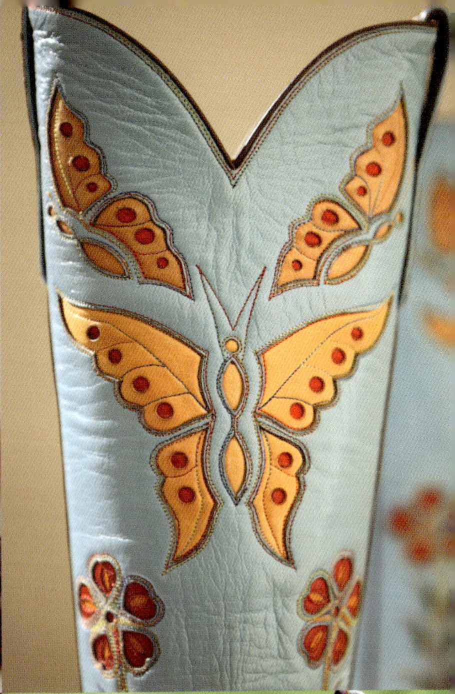
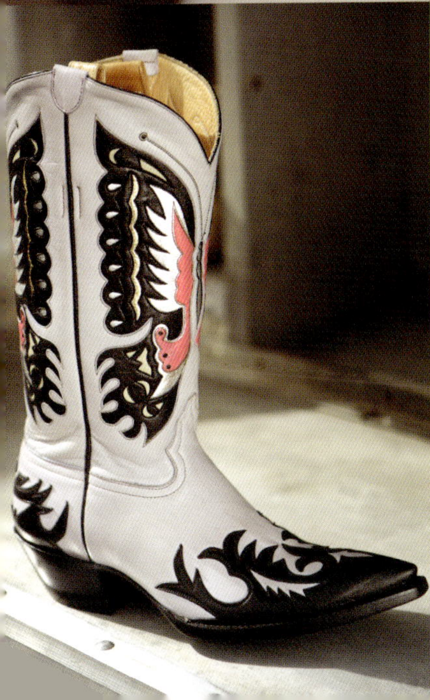
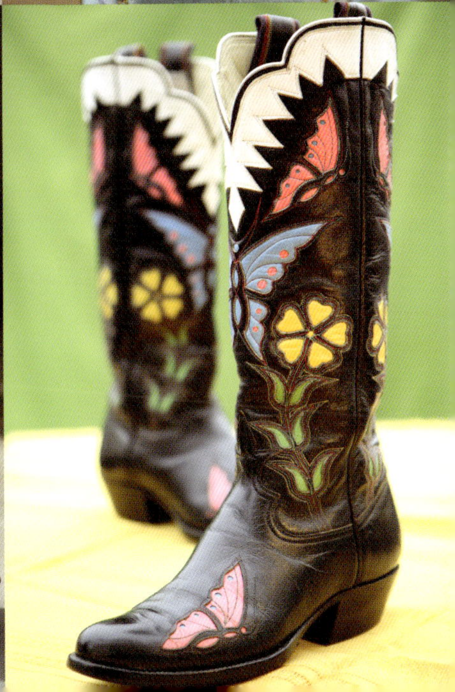

Butterfly collar. Made by Jim Covington; courtesy of Joanie McGrath.

Black butterfly. Made by Custom Boots by Morado; courtesy of John Tongate.

Wingspan. Made by Weinkauf Boots & Leatherworks; courtesy of John Tongate.

Dance hall. These butterfly boots had their soles worn out on West Texas dance floors. The inlay and fancy heel counters are clever choices since partner-dancing women's boots are most often viewed from the back. Made by Willie Lusk; courtesy of Cliff McCall.

"Return to '70s." Made by McGlasson Custom Boots.

almost anywhere on a boot. Placed front and center, the outline of their wings mimics the scallop of the boot top. Other times they land on the foot or vamp and become the most colorful toebug imaginable—though such toes are almost exclusively found on custom boots because of the skill needed to match each toe to the other.

Made from the small leather scraps piled high in most custom boot shops, butterfly wings can be as colorful and intricate as a bootmaker's imagination, and yet sometimes just a simple silhouette is all that's needed to bring to mind the beauty of unbounded space.

Birds

Freedom of movement; speed and grace. Birds on boots are virtually always shown in flight. Western birds mock our fenceposts and barbed wire, for they are not restricted by boundaries or borders.

One of history's most popular and most reproduced boots is the "Blue Bird of Happiness" worn by Gene Autry. They were made by Olsen-Stelzer and were rumored to be the star's favorite pair. Decorated with flying arrows, diamonds, and hearts along the collar and birds soaring upward to cloudlike flowers on the boot top, these colorful boots also have a single-color cutout of a blue bird, which is enough to symbolize the optimism of the West and the man who wore them. In the good ol' days, when trouble stirred, it was nothing that a posse of men carrying guitars couldn't fix with a good ballad. As one of America's most enduring entertainers—the Gene Autry Oklahoma Historical Museum counts "nearly a hundred movies, sixteen years on CBS Radio, more than six hundred records that sold millions (seven gold and two platinum), nearly one hundred television shows, and more than thirty years of personal appearances across the country and overseas"—it is fitting that Autry is remembered by these boots.

Vintage bluebird boots. Made by Malcom; courtesy of Lee and Carrlyn Miller.

Texas birds. The mostly smooth ostrich toe is a sly addition to this pair. Made by Stephanie Ferguson Custom Boots.

Eagle and agave. Maker unknown; courtesy of Evan Voyles.

Yellow bird. Rocketbuster vintage collection.

Monochrome. This abstract butterfly appeared on thousands of Acme cowboy boots. Courtesy of D. Alan Calhoun.

Flight. The golden inlays catch the light; the laces found at each pull catch the wind. Made by McGuffin Custom Boots.

Horse-head counter covers.
Made by Schwarz Custom
Boots; courtesy of Fred Brown.

Ponies and Buffaloes

"Oh, give me a home, where the buffalo roam,
Where the deer and the antelope play;
Where seldom is heard a discouraging word,
And the skies are not cloudy all day."
Brewster Higley, from his poem "My Western Home"

Wild ponies and buffaloes capture the spirit of the untamed West like no other symbols can. Even if these animals are stitched on an otherwise empty boot top, we envision them running free on endless prairies under big skies. Spirited, strong, and swift, these creatures live as many of us would wish to . . . far beyond gates and fences. The only thing that's tame about these cowboy boots is the colors; because even a bright red background can appear too confining, black, brown, and beige are favored because their neutrality leaves more to the imagination.

Stars and Moons

Stars and moons are among the simplest shapes used to symbolize boundless space. A handful of stars and a single crescent moon can turn a plain cowboy boot into an entire night sky. Stars shine as symbols of clarity because they serve as navigation tools. Even those with no knowledge of astronomy instinctively look to the stars to ponder their place in the world.

A crescent moon is nearly always inlaid in white leather and paired with a star. The source of its popularity on work boots may be that the moon is seen in the night sky shortly before sunrise or shortly after sunset, making it a familiar sight to hardworking cowboys on the open range.

Stars and moons are decorations found throughout the West, perhaps most memorably on outhouse doors!

Graffiti boots. "Buffalo Bill's Wild West" is retold in laser-engraved leather. Made by bootmaker Clay Hathaway and Denver-based graffiti artist ACT I, Lonesome Ace Boot Company.

White buffalo. Texas Traditions Boots by Lee Miller; courtesy of Joe Guzzardi.

Stallion. Variation on the rampant or rearing horse with its head uncharacteristically thrown back. Made by Tony Lama, mid-1950s; courtesy of Evan Voyles.

"Plain Freedom." Made by Sorrell Custom Boots; courtesy of Walker Wells.

"Sunset Moonrise." Made by Rocketbuster Boots.

Full moon. Texas Traditions Boots by Lee Miller; courtesy of Joe Guzzardi.

Nighttime bronco. Made by Meanwhile... Back at the Ranch.

Stars and moons. Made by Bob McLean Custom Bootmakers; courtesy of Edward Balogh.

"Plain Freedom" (detail).
Made by Sorrell Custom Boots;
courtesy of Walker Wells.

Coyotes howling. "Ventilated" boots with mesh moon inlays. Made by Stephanie Ferguson Custom Boots.

Native Americans

When stitched on a cowboy boot, an Indian symbolizes both an honorable warrior and a vanishing American frontier.

To this day, the Indians portrayed on cowboy boots are icons, not individuals. The materials and techniques used in bootmaking force simplification, so in almost all cases, Indians are reduced to a feathered headdress. "As shorthand, this one item of apparel, which combines beauty with meaning, became the ultimate symbol of all Indians, even though it has no relevance to many American Indian tribes," according to James Nottage, historian and curator at the Autry National Center.

The feathers of an Indian headdress and the wings of the American eagle are historically significant national symbols, and quite literally two sides of the same coin. From 1859 to 1909, eagles and Indians were imprinted back-to-back on the pennies, nickels, and gold coins carried in the pockets of most Americans.

Unlike butterflies and flowers, which were stitched on cowboy boots as early as the 1920s, Indian-head boots only gained popularity in the 1940s, when intricate inlay on boot tops became available and popular.

For bootmakers, preserving the war bonnet's recognizable shape has proven more important than adhering to realism in other aspects of design and color. Inlaid white feathers were popular, but bolder versions using yellow, black, red, and turquoise were also widespread. Inlaid flying arrows often follow the curve of the boot top and create a sense of movement unlike any other boot design. The Indian figure is always stoic and straight-faced. Much of the success of the headdress design was due to the fact that it was more colorful than eagles, yet more "manly" than butterflies—the headdress was appropriated as a symbol of accomplishment, maturity, and power.

With rising labor costs there was a shift away from inlaid boot styles during the 1960s and 1970s, until, according to Tyler Beard, Tom Cruise's vintage boots hit the big screen in *Top Gun*. What followed was a resurgence of retro-style

"Hopi Specials." Made by McGlasson Custom Boots.

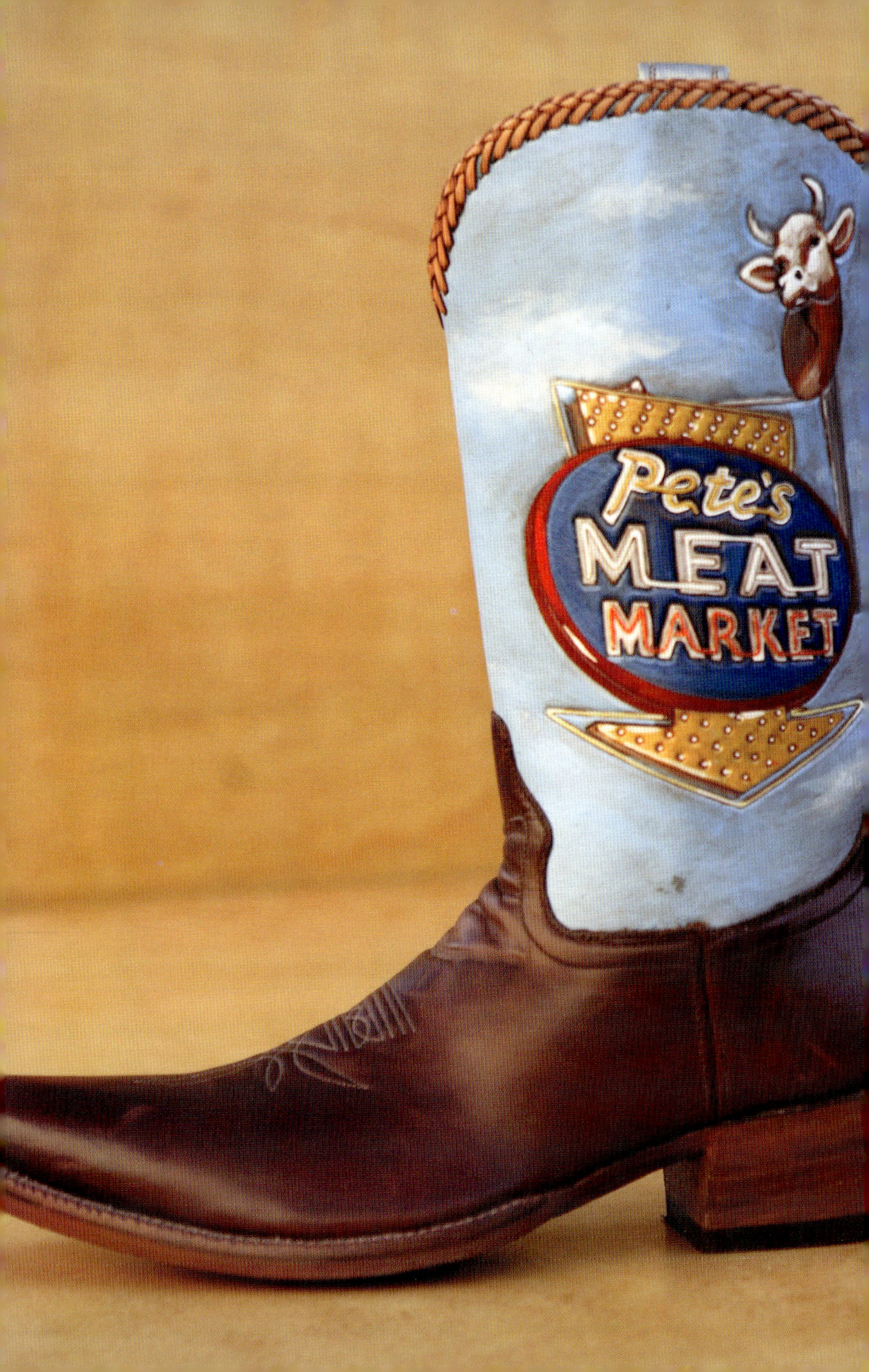
Pete's
MEAT
MARKET

"Roadside America." Rocketbuster Boots updates the Indian-chief motif and simultaneously celebrates the open road with this tooled motel-sign boot top.

Reproduction squash blossom boots. Originally designed long ago by the Las Cruces Boot Company to resemble a Native American necklace design. When customers request that vintage patterns be remade, there is a second chance for innovation. Here, the addition of ostrich skin gives the blue "turquoise" inlay a texture not found in the original. Made by Sorrell Custom Boots; courtesy of Elaine Krankl.

"Avanyu." The olive kangaroo tops feature the winged water serpent from Native American mythology. Made by Sorrell Custom Boots; collection of Dale Sorrell.

Indian chief, buffalo roaming, and crossed arrows. Made by Kimmel Boots; courtesy of Evan Voyles.

Headdress motif. This single boot was found abandoned in a West Texas barn. Rocketbuster vintage collection.

Vintage rattler. Made by Kirkendall Boot Company; collection of Wayne Learned

designs during the mid-1980s, when the vintage boot craze hit urban centers like Los Angeles, New York, and Tokyo. Interest in old patterns was renewed, vintage Indian boots were resoled, and the best examples were remade to satisfy demand.

Custom-made and vintage Indian-head boots remain popular with baby boomers, which is understandable, since this generation spent just as much time in their childhoods playing Indian as they did cowboy. In a way, then, these cowboy boots capture a nostalgic dual personality.

More recently, custom bootmakers are following larger cultural trends. There has been a shift in the portrayal of Native Americans away from warriors and enemies and toward spiritual teachers. These days, bootmakers are filling custom orders for cowboy boots that honor Native American rituals, symbols, and spirituality.

Venomous Critters

Watch where you step! There's danger underfoot! Snakes, spiders, and scorpions—all things that crawl, bite, or sting—seem to work well on boots, no doubt because they relate to the boot's original function. Whatever the danger, the foot is protected, and the wearer can walk with confidence.

A certain degree of realism is required for all "fear factor" boots. Black, brown, and yellow leather provide the necessary camouflage for the boot's element of surprise, and the greatest effect is achieved when the venomous critters are nearly life-sized.

Placement on the boot is important, too: rattlesnakes must be coiled to strike at calf height. Scorpions almost always crawl across the top of the foot. Bootmakers over time have done their best to heighten the effect and frequently stuff cotton padding under the inlay for a more three-dimensional quality.

PAGE 144
top: Scorpion inlay top. Made by Botas Fel-Yni; courtesy of Weasel Bob's Boot Museum. *bottom:* Hand-stitched 3-D scorpions. Made by Little's Boots.
PAGE 145
top: Tarantula. Made by Little's Boots. *bottom:* Diamond-back. Texas Traditions Boots by Lee Miller; courtesy of John Tongate.

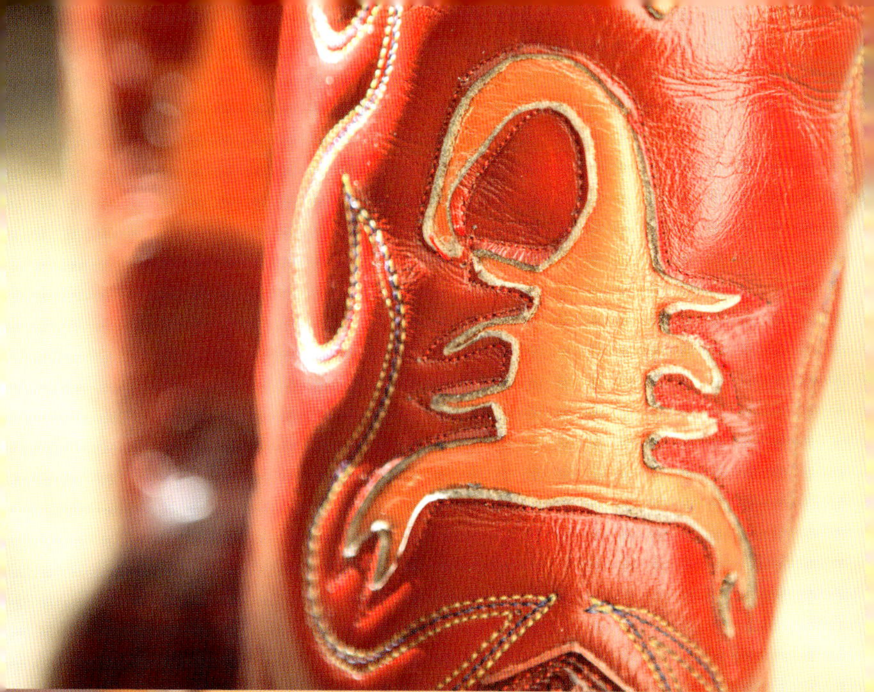

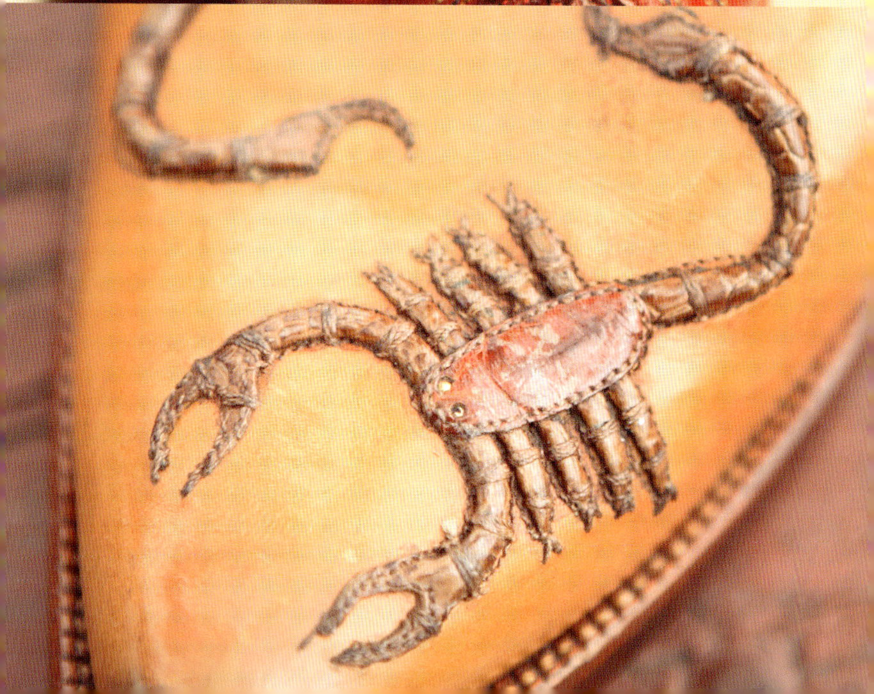

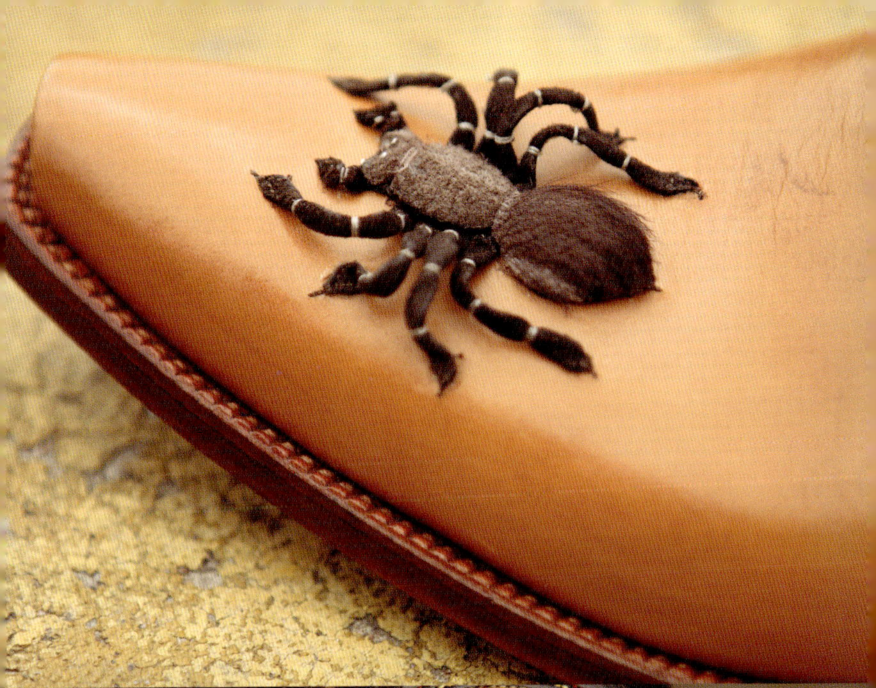

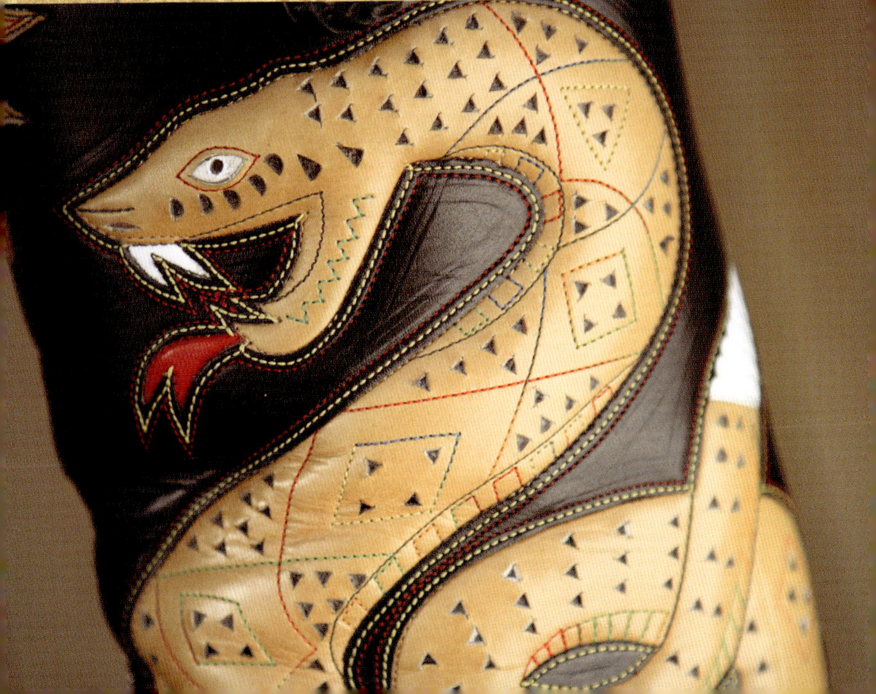

"Rattler Nuevo" (detail). Made by Rocketbuster Boots.

Stinger. Scorpion inlay vamp. Made by Joma Boots; courtesy of Weasel Bob's Boot Museum.

Having the boot pulls so close to the cactus inlay adds a bit of wry humor to this otherwise sophisticated cowboy boot. Made by Jim Covington; courtesy of Paul Blakely.

Cacti

Stitching some cacti on boot tops makes the wearer look extra tough—as if he or she were walkin' on nails. Unlike more fleeting and delicate desert flowers, the cactus is a lasting symbol of survival and endurance.

A cactus can be represented by a simple strip of green leather or it can be much more elaborate. Bootmakers use techniques of inlaying and overlaying leathers to add interest and meaning to their cactus designs.

Thanks to its frequent appearances in the familiar desert backdrops of film and television westerns, the cactus is iconically connected to the rigors of a difficult journey. A single tall saguaro cactus stitched on a cowboy boot can convey the extreme solitude associated with an endless desert.

The prickly pear cactus, with its crowded paddles, represents life's hurdles and man's rugged determination. Star-shaped blossoms of bright pink and yellow add lively spots of color. In ancient Aztec legend, the round red fruit ("tuna") of the nopal cactus symbolizes the human heart.

Cactus needles add mood and meaning, and they are most often sewn as short radiating lines of tiny white stitches. Their angles add energy and attitude to an otherwise still subject.

A well-stitched cactus can be seen as the embodiment of life's hardship and beauty.

Things with a Kick!
Bucking Broncos and Chili Peppers

The American West has always promised to test "what yer made of." Cowboy boots pay special tribute to those willing to take the dare.

The bucking bronco is perhaps the best-known symbol of the American West. The scene frozen in time shows an exciting and wild ride: a cowboy with one hand waving his hat in the air, while the other hand grips the saddle with everything he's got. Some historians believe the horse in the image was modeled after a legendary rodeo horse named Steamboat, who was known for his indomitable spirit.

Needles. This unusual placement of the prickly pear on top of a branch approaches the surreal. Made by Jay Griffith; courtesy of Mark Fletcher.

Prickly pears. Tough red bull hide stitched with Day-Glo thread colors. Made by Tex Robin Boots.

Surrounded. Prickly pear with steer head. Made by Little's Boots.

Cactus ladder. Made by William Shanor.

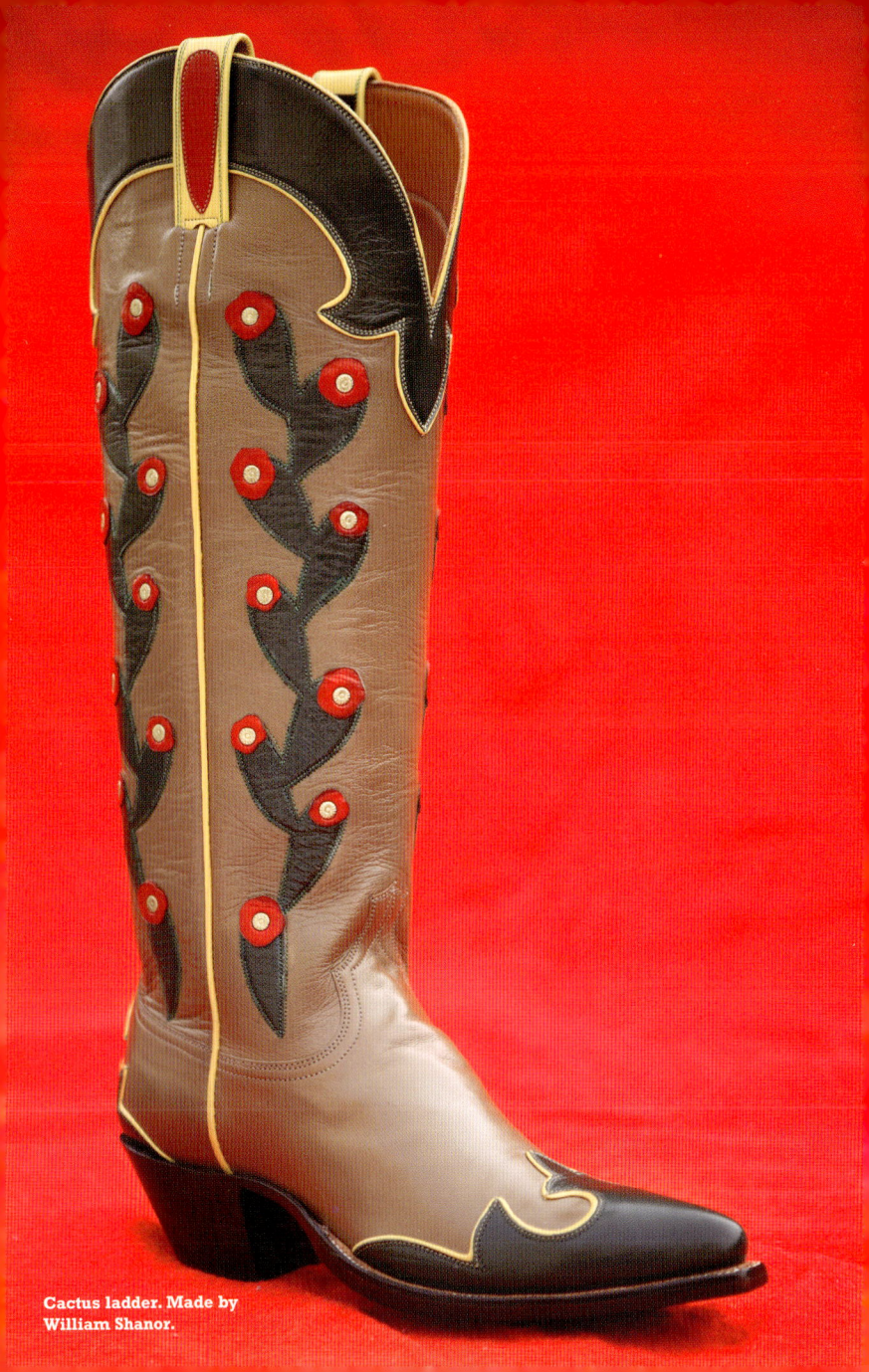

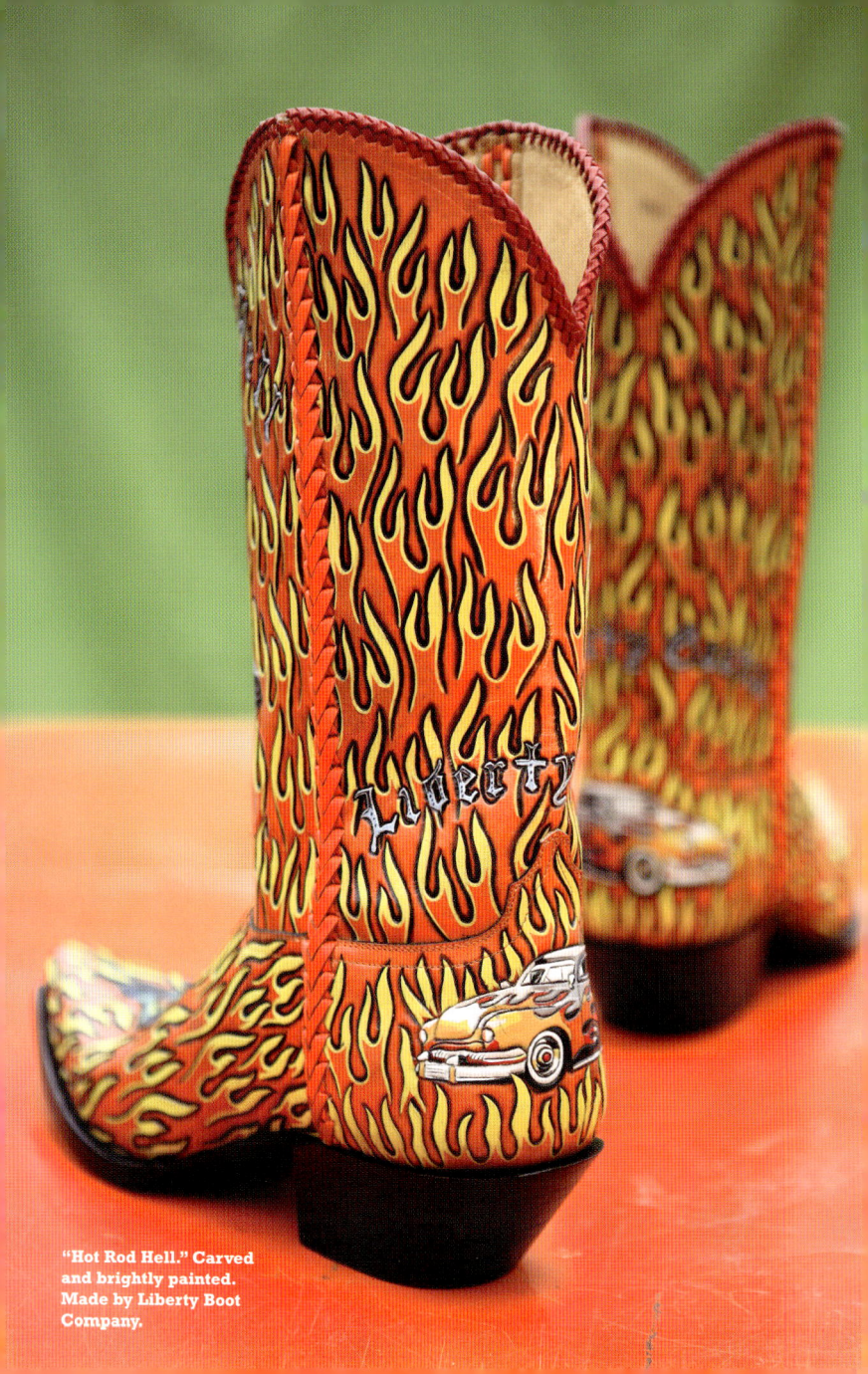

"Hot Rod Hell." Carved and brightly painted. Made by Liberty Boot Company.

Empty saddle. Made by Chris Romero, Don Quixote–brand boot, 1980s; courtesy of Evan Voyles.

Bareback silhouette.
Made by Little's Boots.

"Chili Beauty." Made by Rocketbuster Boots.

Olsen-Stelzer was the first boot company to feature this bucking bronc in its 1940s catalogs, and these boots are now worth thousands of dollars to collectors.

On bronco boots, you're likely to find one man, one unruly horse, and little other decoration.

These cowboy boots remind us to strip away life's clutter and focus on the task at hand. But the rodeo ring isn't the only place you'll find these boots. They are the boots of choice wherever you need to step up to a challenge . . . whether that's in the stirrup, on stage, or in the boardroom. Perhaps more than any others, these boots symbolize conquest.

A milder contest of will, chili peppers present yet another of the West's many challenges. Popularized on custom boots in the 1980s, chili pepper boots pay their respects to Latino culture and the American Southwest, while still conveying potential danger. The long and slightly irregular shape of the chili pepper works well on boot tops, along the toes, or even as pull tabs. The color depends on the wearer's taste: shades of yellow, orange, red, and green in either hot or mild versions.

Whoever wears these boots is making a statement about bravery and suspense.

Skulls and Skeletons

Skulls are cool. Skulls are also tough, serious, edgy, and a widespread fashion icon. The clear-cut morality and "happy trails" of the 1950s have been replaced by growing cultural cynicism and a dark sense of humor. As provocative reminders of the transience of our pleasures and gains, skulls provide a counterweight to lighthearted optimism.

Death represents a metaphoric and inescapable frontier. Its borders are explored through ghost stories, art, trances, and visions.

The 1990s brought us "Day of the Dead" boots, popularized by both Wheeler Boots and Rocketbuster Boots. Black boots with inlays of drinking and guitar-playing skeletons, they are the footwear of choice for shaking off the weight of

The human skull has taken hold as a powerful symbol of modern-day bravado.

Last dance? Made by Back at the Ranch.

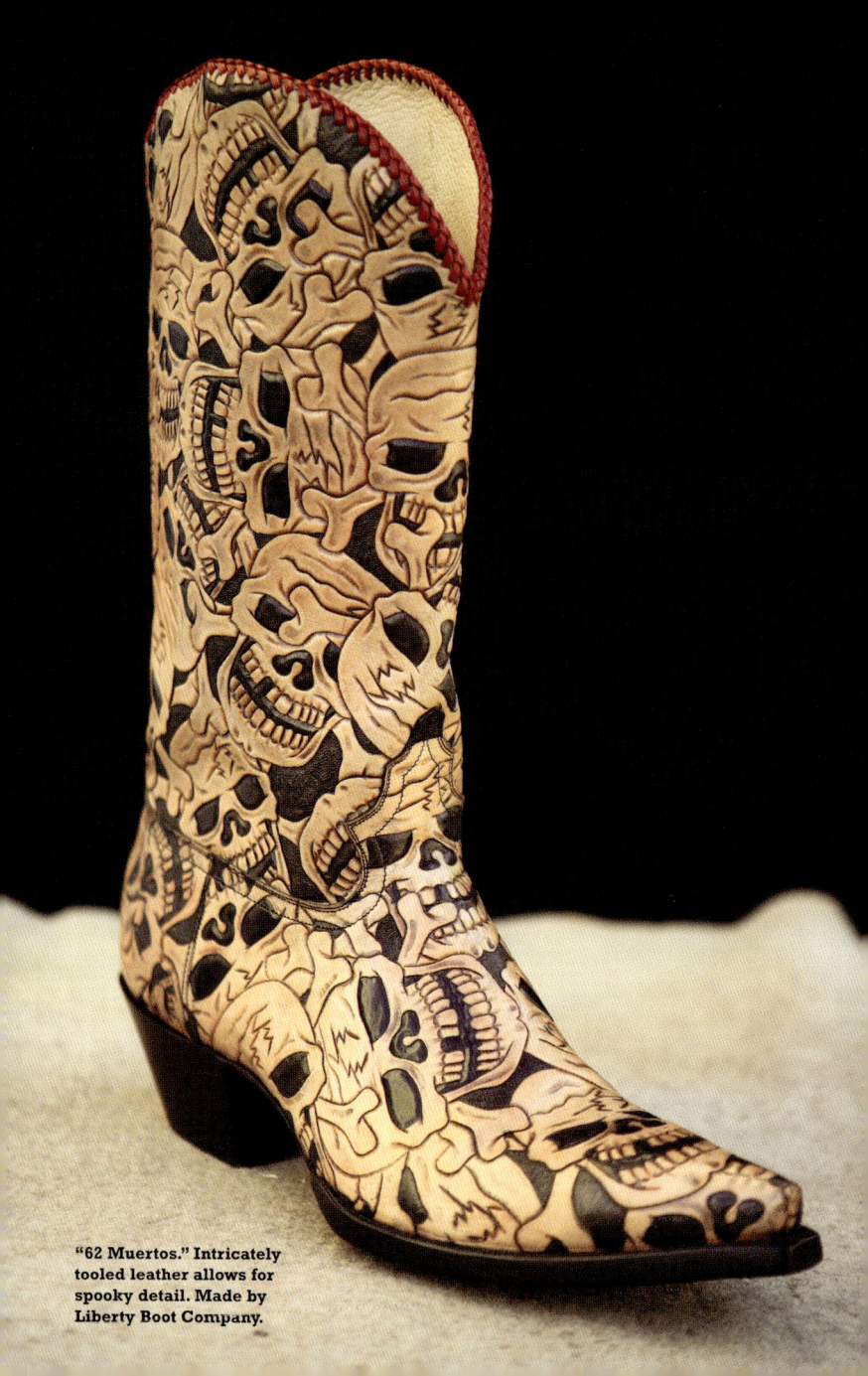

"62 Muertos." Intricately tooled leather allows for spooky detail. Made by Liberty Boot Company.

Boots with skull motifs often incorporate other design elements, like helmets and tusks, to heighten the sense of danger or dread. Made by Riff Raff Leatherworks.

THIS PAGE
"Big Devil" (with silver charm inlay). Made by Liberty Boot Company.
OPPOSITE PAGE
top left: "Brody Rocks." Made by Liberty Boot Company. *top right:* "Killaz Pee Wees." Made by Liberty Boot Company. *bottom right:* Some decorated heel counters send a "kiss my ass" message. Made by Liberty Boot Company. *bottom left:* "Day of the Dead." Made by Rocketbuster Boots.

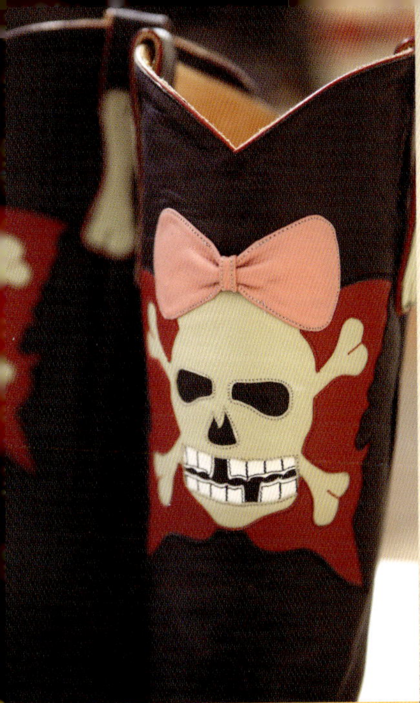
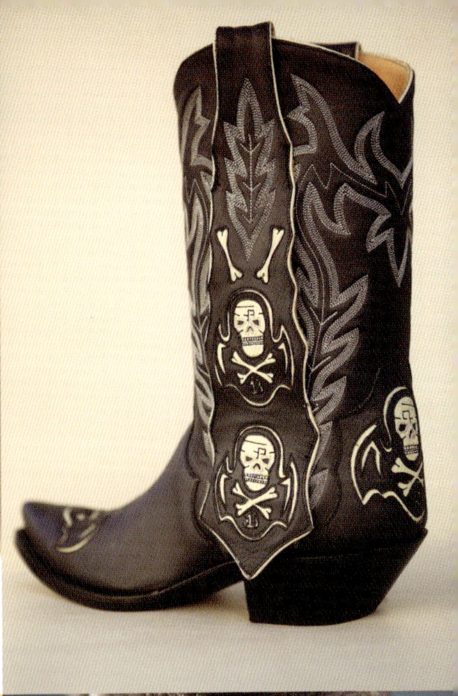
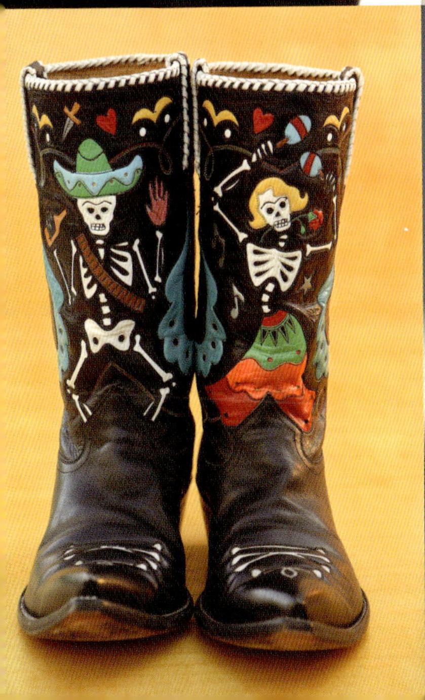
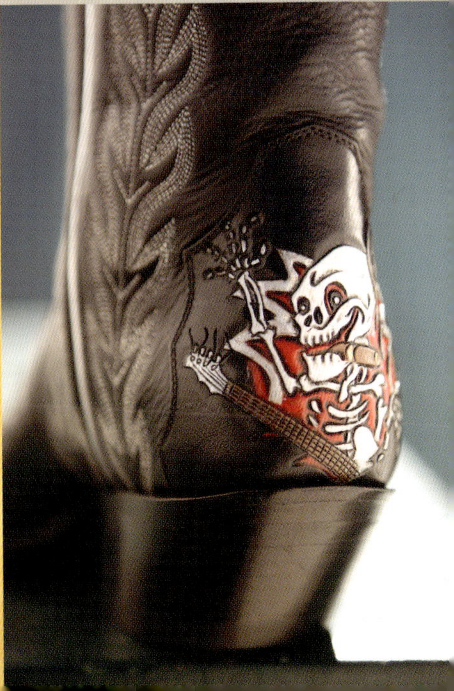

Foiled leather evokes crystalline sugar skulls and paper cutouts. With one skeleton on each boot, the two move and dance independently. Made by McGuffin Custom Boots.

the world and for dancing on top of graves. These boots mock death as little more than a simple inconvenience, and they even celebrate it as ultimately liberating.

"The word 'death' is not pronounced in New York, in Paris, in London because it burns the lips. The Mexican, by contrast, is familiar with death . . . jokes about it, caresses it, sleeps with it, celebrates it; it is one of his favorite toys and his most steadfast love."
Octavio Paz, *The Labyrinth of Solitude*

Cowboy, rebel, outlaw . . . each accepts his fate. Death is a border we cross alone. None of us gets the benefit of a posse.

"No matter how I struggle and strive I'll never get out of the world alive."
Lyrics to "I'll Never Get Out of This World Alive"
(Hank Williams and Fred Rose)

The human brain is hardwired to find and recognize a human face, even in its most rudimentary form. Skeletal silhouettes of the eyes, nose, and a few broken teeth have a primitive appeal that make skulls—human and critter—a desired motif on boot tops. There may even come a time when skulls are as common on cowboy boots as butterflies, but for now they still carry considerable shock value.

Catering to those who think life's too short to wait for custom boots, Liberty Boot Company integrates hard rockin' images of skulls, guitars, and flames into boot designs whose message is one of passion and immortality.

Luck and Chance

"You gotta play to win."
Nationwide lottery slogan

"Going west" has always meant taking chances, and gambling has been a favorite form of entertainment for those on the frontier. Easy come, easy go. Every game is a new beginning.

Horseshoes, playing cards, dice, and even slot machines are popular subjects for cowboy boot inlay. They are worn by those who look forward to the excitement of the game and who know that winning's never a sure thing. These boots are favored by optimists, entrepreneurs, and Hollywood celebrities. All any of us needs is one lucky break.

"Lucky boots" are often visually crammed with good-luck charms like four-leaf clovers, lucky sevens, gold coins, and horseshoes. The symbols are usually so intricate and numerous that they look like tightly fitted puzzle pieces.

Brand-new luck-themed cowboy boots can have a vintage feel because these symbols of both good fortune and bad have long been familiar. Each color used for these lucky boots—red, black, white, green, gold, silver—conveys a meaning and all symbolize the "payout."

"If it wasn't for luck, I'd win every time."
Phil Hellmuth, World Series of Poker star

In American mythology, gamblers are admired as "outsiders," skilled and self-reliant enough to take a chance on beating the odds. Scornful of the drudgery of conventional hard work, they take risks in order to get ahead.

Poker has evolved from a Wild West pastime to a popular televised "sport." Every player is on an even footing, each player is dealt a hand; individual success is a matter of luck and skill, and sometimes a really good bluff. Sound familiar? Why it's nothing less than the American dream.

Motif and Metaphor

Playing cards show up on many cowboy boots. The most popular is the "Aces & Eights" or "Dead-Man's Hand," made famous as the hand Wild Bill Hickok was holding when he was shot to death during a poker game in Deadwood, South Dakota. Although it seems certain that Wild Bill was holding a pair of black aces and another pair of black eights, the fifth card is up for debate. To this day, there are superstitious card players who will refuse to play if dealt that particular hand.

As the world speeds up, so have the games we play. Slot machines and other casino games promise mega jackpots. Dice, flames, and hot-rod pinstriping celebrate the risks—and rewards—that are part of any high-stakes pursuit.

Prosperity

"Cattle and oil wells. That's what they smell like to you. They smell like money to us."
www.texasnative.com

Land. Gold. The glitz and allure of Hollywood. People go west to find or make their fortunes. For Americans, the West has always promised opportunity, freedom, and ultimately, prosperity. And with every boom and bust, the symbols of prosperity change.

Many time-honored icons of striking it rich, such as oil derricks and longhorns, have taken on an air of nostalgia. Personal fortunes are now made in real estate, media, and technology. The logos relating to new money are often too short-lived, too literal, or too abstract to make a lasting contribution to the iconographic vocabulary of wealth.

Symbols of prosperity, reinforced by the use of exotic and costly materials, make sense on cowboy boots. Custom-built boots are in and of themselves a luxury, so when a wearer lifts his cuff to reveal an oil well, it merely underscores his success and gives us a glimpse of the "happy ending" we all hope for.

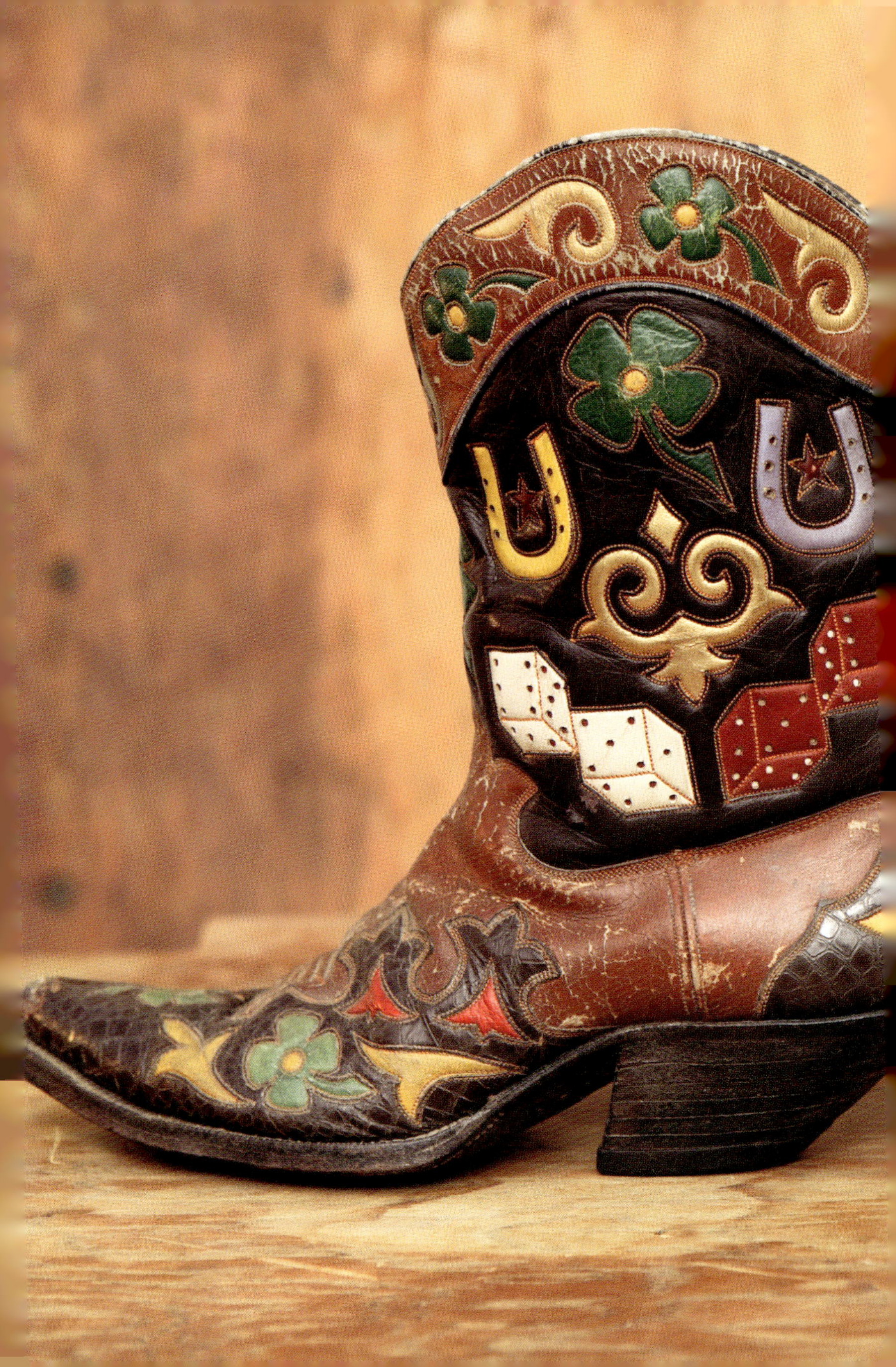

Lots o' Luck, 1940s. The Dixon brothers (Noble and Andy) made boots for many country-and-western stars of the 1950s, most notably Lefty Frizzell. They were accustomed to doing fancy work, and the dice and cards seen here were stock Dixon inlay patterns; courtesy of Evan Voyles.

Lucky 21. Made by Tex Robin Boots; collection of James Willett.

Good luck. Angel boots with gold linings. Made by James Leddy Boot Company; courtesy of Jeff Borins.

"Welcome to Vegas." Made by Tres Outlaws.

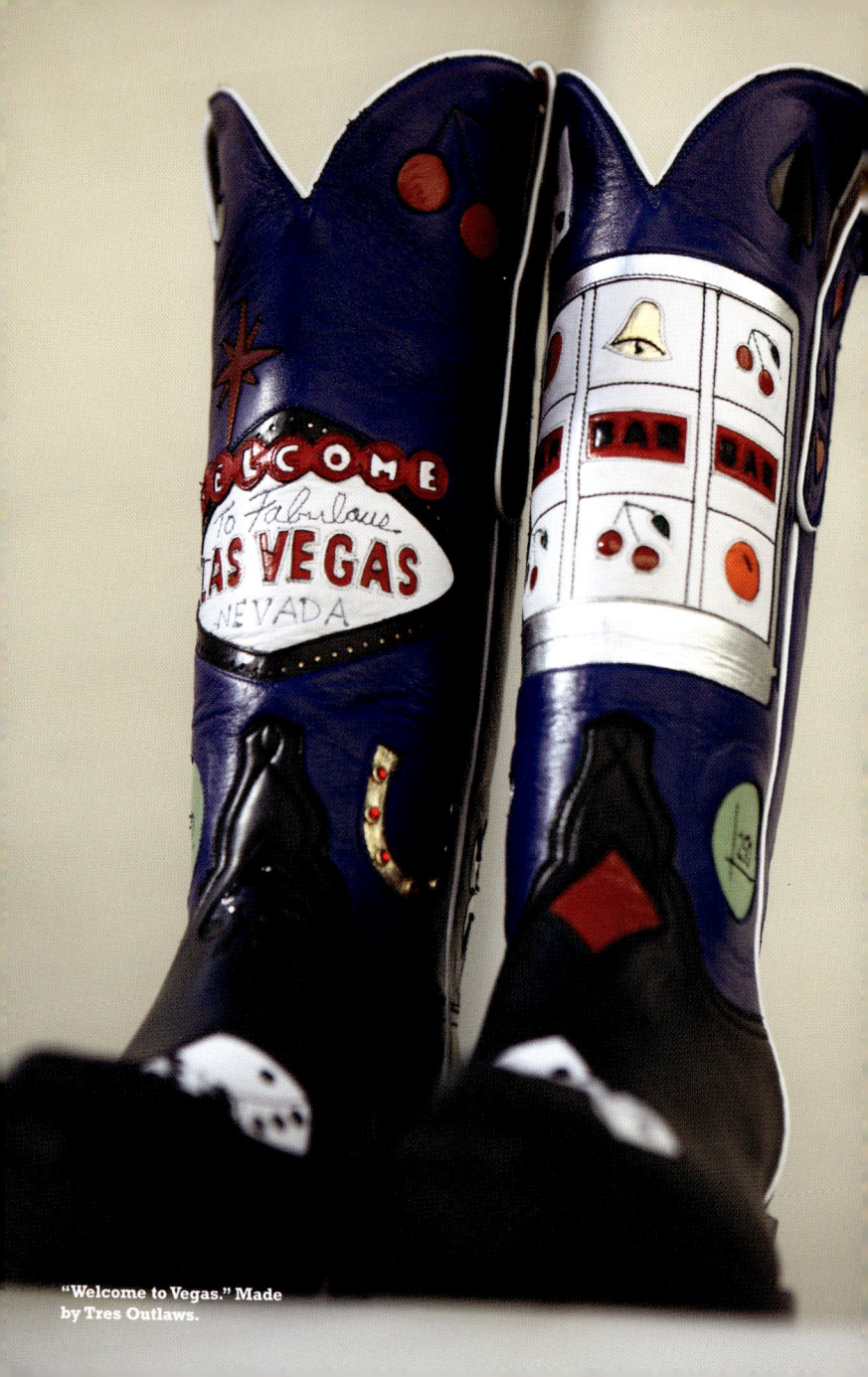

Shining diamond inlay, 1970s. Made by Charlie Dunn, Texas Traditions; courtesy of Evan Voyles.

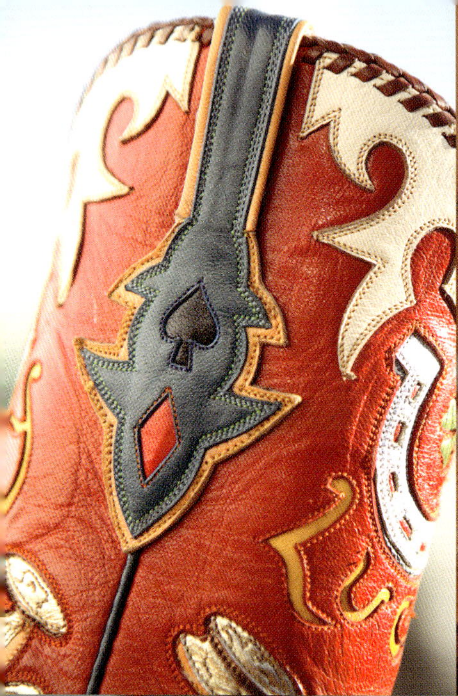
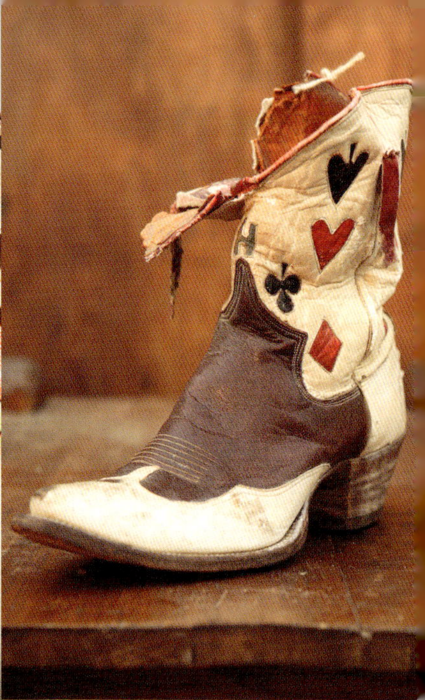
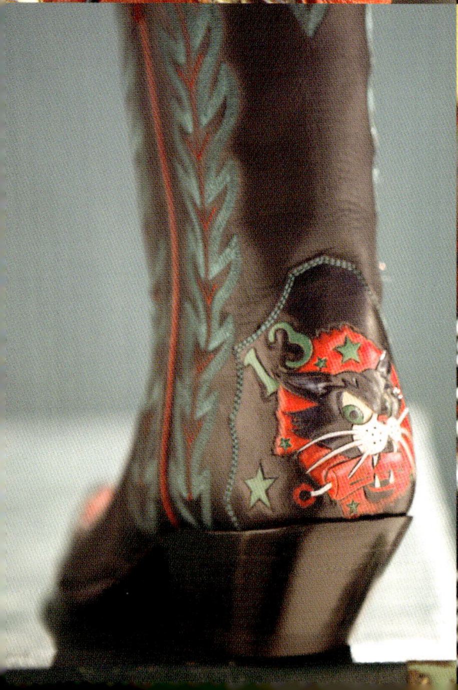
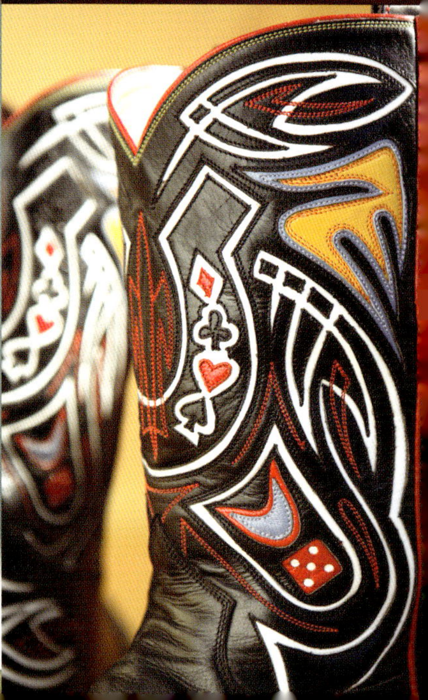

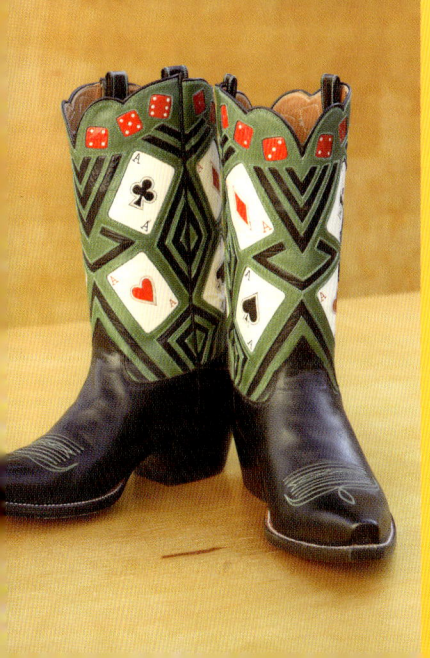

THIS PAGE
top left: "Kickin' Clovers."
top right: "Golden Horseshoe." *bottom left:* "High Roller." All made by Rocketbuster Boots.
OPPOSITE PAGE
top left: "Lucky." Made by Rocketbuster Boots. *top right:* Marked cards. Made by Hakey Boot Company, 1940s; courtesy of Evan Voyles. *bottom right:* "Octane." Made by Rocketbuster Boots. *bottom left:* Cigar kitty. Whether it's 'cuz you figure you've got nothing to lose, or you're just using reverse psychology to improve your fate, these "bad luck" boots carry the "Lucky 13" and a black cat with a short fuse. Made by Liberty Boot Company.

"Lucky Charms." Made by Rocketbuster Boots.

Irony is seldom found on cowboy boots. This pair is rich with meaningful details. Cattle, cotton, and oil—these "boom and bust boots" tell the hard-luck story of many small towns in Texas. The past glory associated with longhorns, white cotton, and gushing oil wells is depicted on the back of the boots. The rough-out toes point to a Texas gone bust, where the rhythmic motion of the pump jack is now still. Nothing lasts forever. Made by Kimmel Boots and owned by Evan Voyles.

> **"Other states were carved or born;
> Texas grew from hide and horn."**
>
> Berta Hart Nance, from her poem "Cattle"

Longhorns

Images of longhorn cattle have long appeared on cowboy boots as symbols of western prosperity. A breed all their own, wearers of these boots are a headstrong bunch and known to grab life by the horns. When circumstances demand it, they tackle a rough road and head boldly toward what lies ahead.

Longhorns are descended from cattle brought to the Americas by Christopher Columbus in 1493 and later tended by Mexican vaqueros. By 1867, longhorn cattle began to resemble stampeding dollar signs. Cattle worth four dollars a head for their hide and tallow in Texas sold for ten times that amount when delivered to Joe McCoy at the railhead in Abilene, Kansas.

Early cowboys rounded up millions of cattle that roamed the open range. Abandoned when Texans left to fight in the Civil War, left to stray and multiply, these cattle were free for the taking. (Many others, however, were stolen from Mexican ranchers.)

Longhorn cattle stand for strength, power, and virility. A wild and sometimes unpredictable breed, the longhorn required early cowboys to ride with a gun on their hip. Perfectly suited to grazing the harsh terrain on the range, longhorns are the only cattle that actually gain weight during a long cattle drive, thus turning them into potent symbols of prosperity in times of boom or bust.

Much wider than it is tall, the silhouette of a longhorn is, ironically, the wrong shape for a cowboy boot. But through sheer will, determination, and design ingenuity, the longhorn has been stitched on so many pairs that it has become one of the images most strongly associated with cowboy boots. And since cowhide remains the most critical and popular material in bootmaking, longhorn designs aptly tie together message and material.

In 1927, there were fewer longhorn cattle than American bison—due not to slaughter but to breeding with more docile ranch-style breeds. Brought back from the edge of extinction, longhorns symbolize a tough, sturdy breed of westerner—a true survivor.

Motif and Metaphor

Gold foil leather has been used by bootmakers since the 1950s to imply wealth and glamour. Made by Young's Custom Boots.

These wild-eyed longhorns are the central characters in an overall great boot design. Although the inlay is rather simple, the repetition of "points" among the eyes, horns, stars, moon, and stitching give a thorny, ornery quality to these late-1940s boots. Made by Rios Boot Company; courtesy of Byron Barr.

Lasso. A red-stamped longhorn gives this vintage child's boot the playful look of a Cracker Jack prize. Maker unknown; courtesy of D. Alan Calhoun.

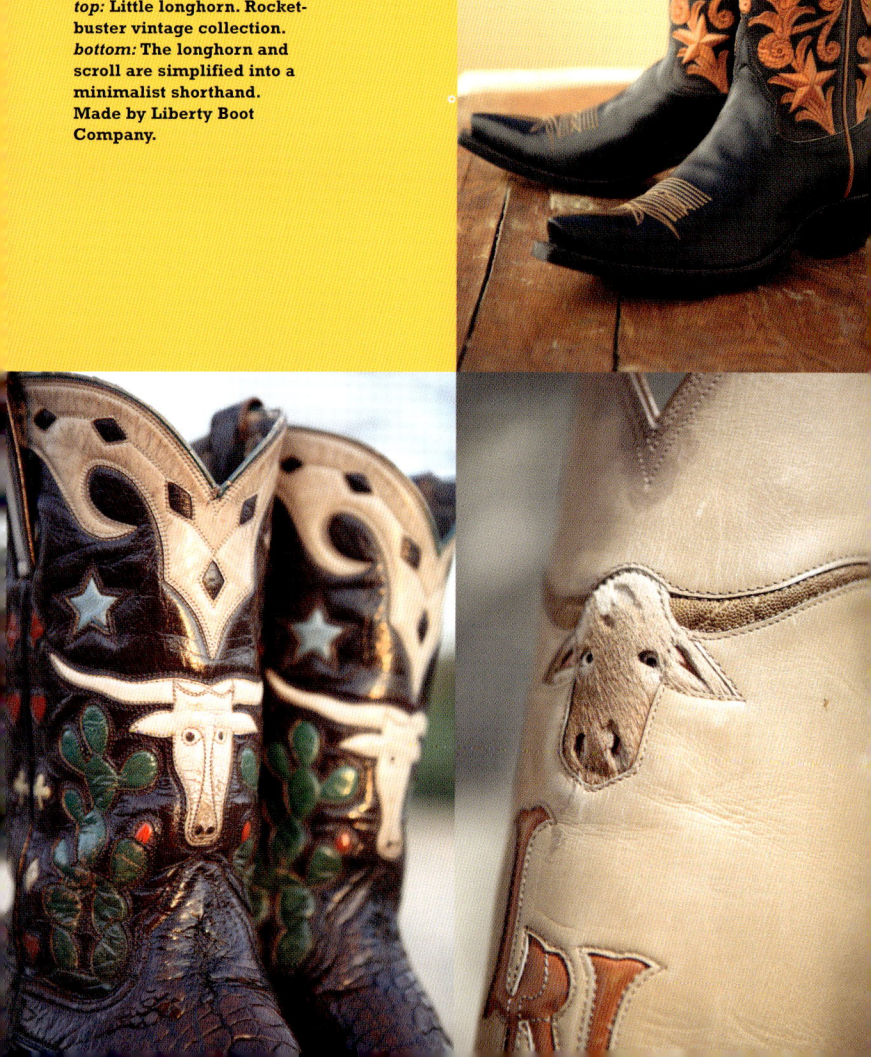

THIS PAGE
top right: Tooled longhorn and stars. Made by Back at the Ranch. *bottom right:* This longhorn with elephant inlay for the horns and hair-on hide resembles tiny taxidermy. Made by Charlie Dunn, Texas Traditions; courtesy of Lee and Carrlyn Miller. *bottom left:* Gramps. Made by Little's Boots.
OPPOSITE PAGE
top: Little longhorn. Rocketbuster vintage collection. *bottom:* The longhorn and scroll are simplified into a minimalist shorthand. Made by Liberty Boot Company.

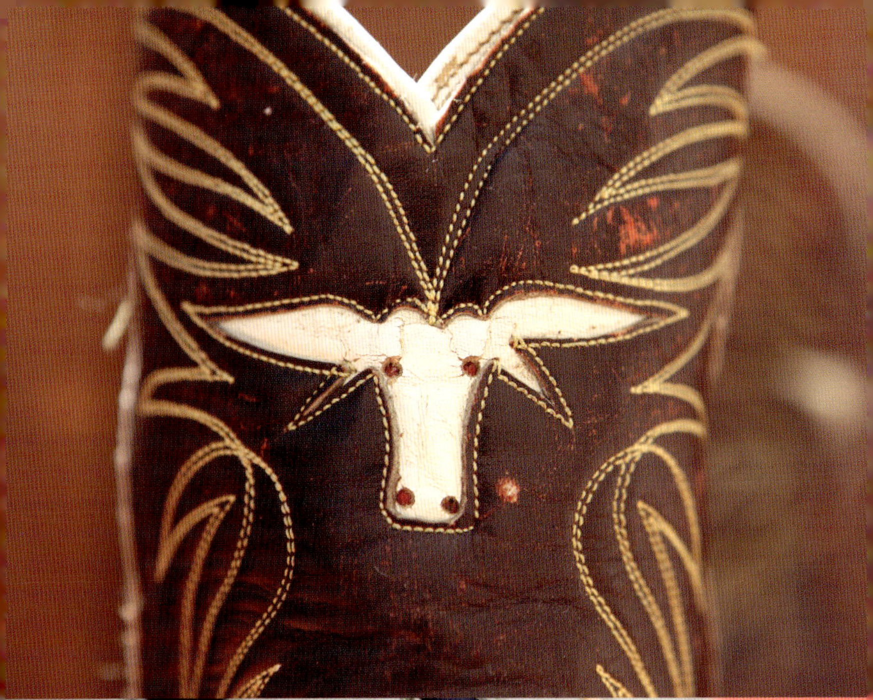
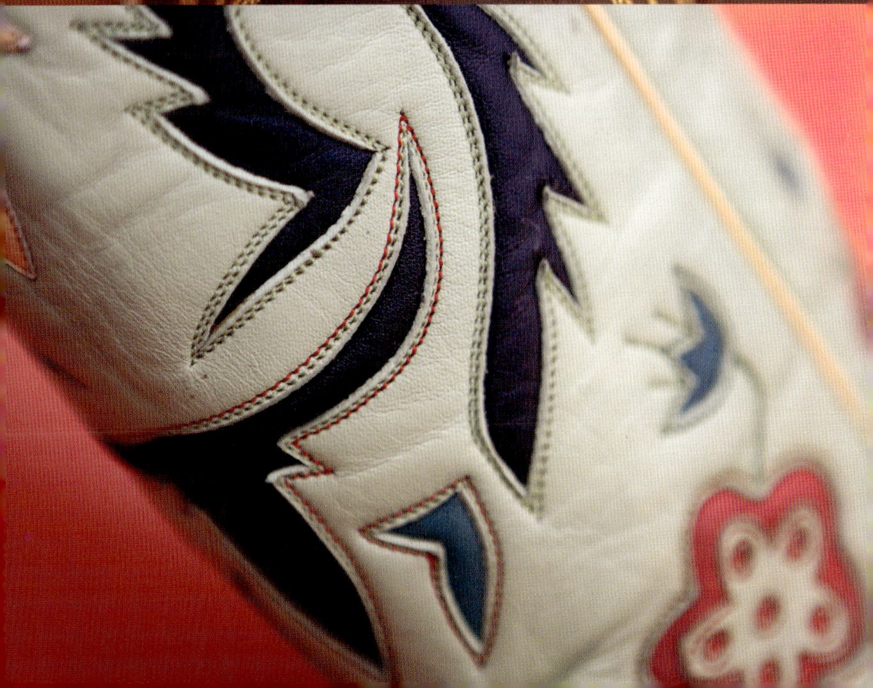

Longhorns and pistols.
Rocketbuster vintage
collection.

Carved leather inlay
and yellow buck stitching.
Made by Liberty Boot
Company.

Despite its popularity, the wide shape of the longhorn is rather awkward on a boot. Here bootmaker Carl Chappell wisely placed the longhorn near the top, implying the presence of a scallop. The white stitched toebug also provides balance to the design. Made by C.T. Boot Shop; courtesy of John Tongate.

Barbed wire. Made by Caboots.

Hand-tooling provides the realistic and expressive detail that inlays cannot. Bootmaker Carl Chappell once built and carved a pair of boots featuring an entire cattle drive on the tops.

Barbed Wire and Fences

Between 1866 and 1890, there were more than ten million cattle driven north from Texas. Once the railroad arrived in the Southwest, the cattle drive era was over, and Texans turned to ranching—and barbed wire.

Patented in 1874 by J. F. Glidden, barbed wire changed the landscape of the West. Where earlier fences kept roaming livestock *out* of farmers' crops, barbed wire was meant to keep cattle penned *in*. Barbed wire became an early symbol of civilization, of the conquest and possession of space, and of commerce and progress.

Barbed wire is an example of a symbol that has a new meaning in today's world. It is stitched on cowboy boots in pieces, alone as a symbol, without the context of livestock and property. Where once it meant "conquest," it now implies "escape."

Oil Derricks

"Formula for success: Rise early, work hard, strike oil."

J. Paul Getty, founder of the Getty Oil Company

The meaning of the oil derrick on cowboy boots is clear: it's all about striking it rich.

On January 10, 1901, at Spindletop oil field near Beaumont, Texas, the Gladys City Oil, Gas and Manufacturing Company struck oil and made history. The gusher spewed oil a hundred feet into the air for nine days before it was capped. It went on to produce an estimated hundred thousand barrels a day. That gushing oil well was viewed worldwide as a harbinger of wealth in a new industrial age.

Gusher. Made by Duck Menzies Bootmaker; courtesy of Hugh Roberson.

Barbed wire is a repetitive decorative pattern that also conveys history and meaning. Made by Tex Robin Boots; courtesy of Mark Fletcher.

Oil derrick. The shiny black vamp on this boot looks like slick black crude. Made by Little's Boots.

"Lil' Buckaroo." These longhorn boots show a split-rail fencing rather than barbed wire—an almost suburban sense of "home." Made by Rocketbuster Boots.

Exotic. Boots embellished with medallions carved from fossilized mammoth ivory. Made by Stallion Boot Company.

> Claim owners were sometimes slow to cap big wells because they believed that the sight of gushing oil would attract eager investors.

An oil frenzy quickly spread across Texas, promising unimaginable wealth for landowners and jobs for everyone else. As oil workers and their families moved in, small farming towns underwent population explosions that changed them forever.

Just as oil replaced cattle on the Texas landscape, oil wells soon replaced longhorns on boot tops. Visually distinctive, oil derricks were stitched in all their elaborate structural detail during the late 1940s and early 1950s. Nocona produced an oil-well boot in which the inlaid derrick was gold metallic leather, making the metaphor explicit.

Oil derrick boots are still popular, custom made by Texas bootmakers as odes to a previous generation or in gratitude for a family fortune made in oil or for the hard work of relatives in the oil fields.

Glamour

"I do not make clothes. I make images."
Manuel, Nashville clothier

In the past ten years, there has been a renaissance of the glamorous cowboy boot thanks to makers such as Tres Outlaws, Stallion Boot Company, and Rocketbuster Boots, and to select smaller shops like Lisa Sorrell and JP's Custom Handmade Boots.

There are fancy boots, and then there are *glamorous* boots. Margaret Farrand Thorp, author of *America at the Movies*, defines glamour as "sex appeal plus luxury plus elegance plus romance." It is a celebration of form over function, and like many couture gowns on a fashion runway, there are a number of boots that teeter on the edge of unwearable because of their narrow heels—and the trail of glittering rhinestones they leave behind.

High heels and pointed toes are the makings of sex appeal. High cowboy or fashion heels realign the wearer's body: the stomach tucks in and the booty sticks out. Extreme heels of three and four inches send a message of pure fun: less function, more flash.

Luxury starts with a boot's custom fit and is then exaggerated with expensive exotic materials and labor-intensive detailing. Intricate inlay requires thoughtful design work and flawless cutting, skiving, and stitching.

Exotic leathers like crocodile and stingray provide a high gloss sheen that grabs the attention of passersby.

Exquisite cowboy boots can require the careful coordination of hundreds of tiny details. Creating a symmetry not normally found in nature, a handful of custom bootmakers will meticulously match the tile size and placement of a crocodile skin so that the right and left boots are a perfectly matched pair.

The only thing more expensive than alligator hide is craftsmanship. Intricate inlay, leather tooling, and hand-cut lacing all add to a boot's handmade appeal. Embellishments like sterling silver toe caps, bootpull buckles, and heels are precious not only because of the metals themselves, but also because of the skill required to handcraft and engrave them.

A sure sign of luxury is when the number of hours required to make the boots far exceeds the number of hours the boots are likely to be worn. Many of Tres Outlaws's tooled boots routinely require four hundred to six hundred hours of work to design, tool, ink, and build.

In the 1950s, labor costs exceeded the combined costs of leather and thread for all large U.S. boot companies. The main difference between today's custom boots and the intricate vintage boots made from 1945 to 1955, during the golden age of inlay, is that today skilled labor will cost you dearly.

Many of the most glamorous boots of the late 1950s and 1960s were made by Nudie of Hollywood. Nudie outfitted country and western stars like Roy Rogers, Dale Evans, Rex Allen, Buck Owens, Dolly Parton, and countless others. These cowboy boots were most often made to complement suits made entirely from gold lamé and accented with rhinestones. The outfits, including the boots, were meant to dazzle crowds

Motif and Metaphor

> Once rhinestones were reserved for Grand Ole Opry and rodeo stars. Today, "bling" has made a big comeback across a wide social spectrum.

from any stage, rodeo arena, or parade route. The heels of Nudie-made boots are often wrapped with leather and encrusted with rhinestones to match the boot top.

Stage boots can often be spotted by a quick look at their soles. Cemented on, trimmed close to the foot, and with no surrounding stitch, these soles make a boot lighter and sleeker looking.

Anyone with money and imagination can own a spectacular pair of cowboy boots. You'll find these high-style boots dressing attendees to fundraisers, film festivals, and inaugurations. Santa Fe's Buckaroo Ball inspires guests to try and outdo both last year's cowboy boots and charitable giving. The Golden Boot Awards dinner, given by the Motion Picture & Television Fund, celebrates the past and present of the Hollywood western.

Governor Arnold Schwarzenegger is rumored to own more than one hundred pairs of boots. Many of his boot tops carry the California governor's seal and hand-applied details like lacing and tooled leather vamps. His bootmaker, Tres Outlaws, balances the power implied by the seal and the weight of the top design with the counterweight of handmade silver toe tips and heel caps, along with gold inlay. In many ways, Schwarzenegger epitomizes the American dream as he continually reinvents himself: bodybuilder, actor, politician. His boots are dignified, glamorous, and definitely kick-ass.

"Feeling and longing are the motive forces behind all human endeavor and human creations."

Albert Einstein, physicist

With layer upon layer of handwork and precious materials, the only thing missing from glamorous boots is a sense of what's to come. Whereas plainer cowboy boots point to adventure that lies ahead, this category of boot has all the look and feel of having arrived at a *very* happy ending.

"Buckaroo Ball." Made by Rocketbuster Boots.

Tiny personal symbols play hide-and-seek in hand-carved scrolls. Custom-made by Tres Outlaws for Senator John Kerry.

"Rhinestone cowboy," late 1950s/early 1960s. Most Nudie boots of this period have a two-tone color scheme that matched a custom-made suit and/or saddle. This boot has unique accents in a third color. Made by Nudie's; courtesy of Evan Voyles.

Matching crocodile wingtip. Made by Stallion Boot Company.

Gemstone. Spots of genuine turquoise. Boots by Tres Outlaws.

"Ruby Red." Made by Rocketbuster Boots.

Religion

"Lord, when trails are steep and passes high, Help me ride it straight the whole way through."
Roy Rogers, cowboy actor, singer, and performer

In the early West, there were few established churches, and Sunday was considered by many as just another work day. God's grace and creative force were seen in every cloud, crop, critter, and acre of prairie.

Religious cowboy boots are often humble tributes. They are reminders, with every step, to stay true to one's chosen path.

Patriotism

Cowboy boots stitched with stars, stripes, and eagles convey powerful cultural messages. Like the American flag itself, these cowboy boots symbolize pride, unity, and freedom.

You can print a flag on a coffee mug, but it simply won't carry the myth and significance of a flag on a cowboy boot. Boots enjoy a sense of history and purpose that makes them a perfect vehicle for patriotic showmanship.

Eagles

Before there were flags on boots, there were eagles. The eagle is a ubiquitous national symbol, found on coins, currency, and buildings. Popular not just with Americans, this noble bird also represents such nations as Mexico, Germany, Austria, Poland, Syria, and Indonesia.

For many of the same design reasons, eagles are as well-suited as butterflies for placement on boot tops. The eagle is commonly depicted with its wings spread, showing its strength and majesty. The eagle's wingspan can stretch to fill a boot top of any height. The intricacies of the feathers show off a bootmaker's skill as few other motifs can.

Eagle boots were insanely popular during the early 1950s, in large part because of the patriotism and prosperity following World War II, but also because of major western

"Cowboy Church" is held Sunday mornings outside many small towns and inside many rodeo arenas. Worshippers are asked to "Come as you are" to enjoy music and fellowship.

OPPOSITE
"The Madonna of Sorrows." Made by Lariat Gang Boots & Shoes; courtesy of Debbie Taylor.

Motif and Metaphor

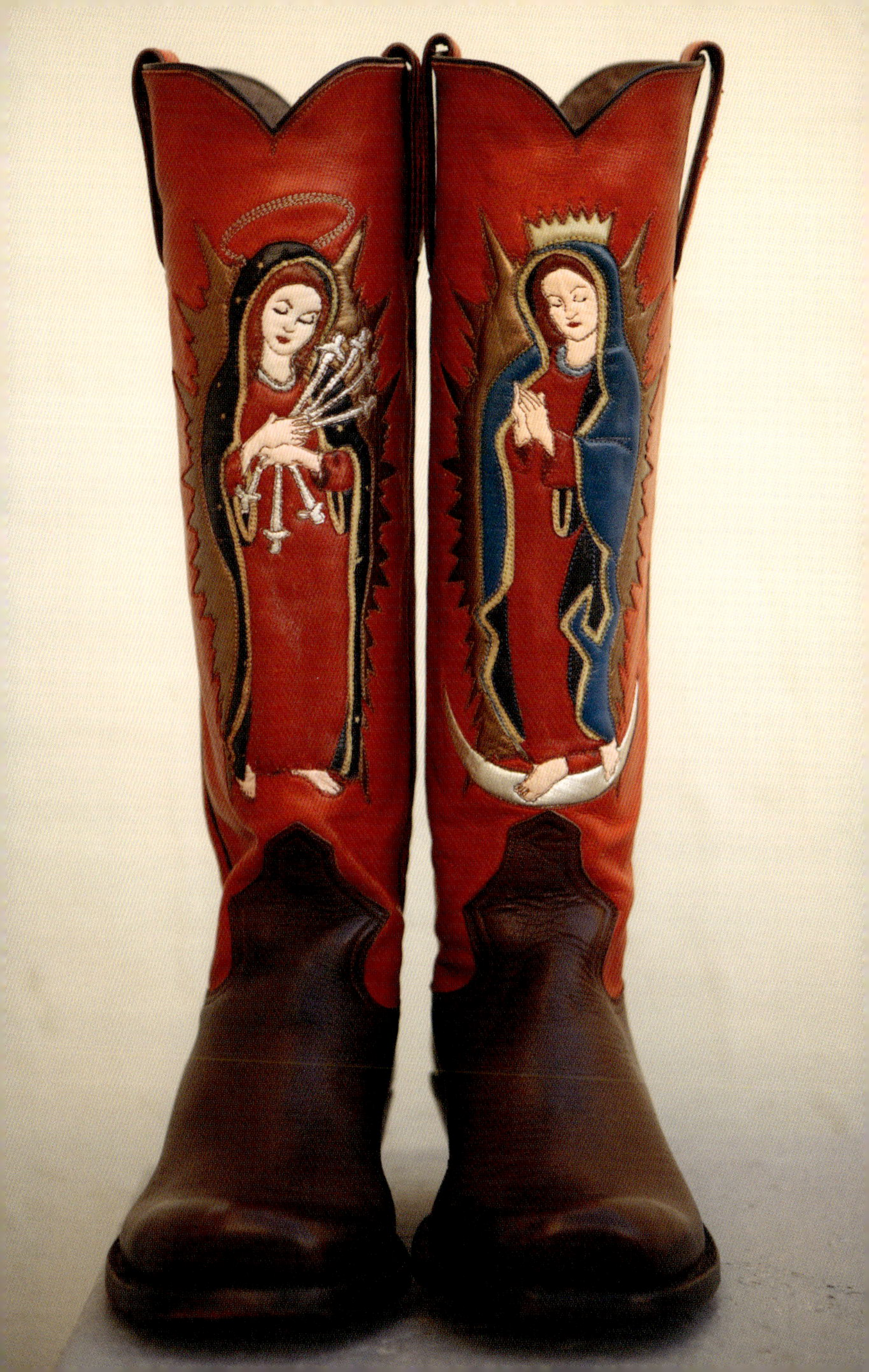

Romans 10:15: "How beautiful are the feet of them that preach the gospel of peace..." Made by Spikes Custom Boots; courtesy of Ryan Fraser.

"Virgin Guadalupe." Made by Rocketbuster Boots.

Eagle wingtip. Made by Kimmel Boots; courtesy of Bryce Sunderlin.

Custom-made brown eagles, 1940s. Made by Lucchese Boot Company; courtesy of Lee and Carrlyn Miller.

Tufted feather eagle.
Rocketbuster vintage
collection.

Silver foil. The twisted leather or "gill work" makes for a more realistic feathered look. Made by McGuffin Custom Boots.

Laurels. Made by Riff Raff Leatherworks; courtesy of Lemmy Kilmister of the band Motörhead.

Simple eagle. Rocketbuster vintage collection.

Mexican-inspired, the colors have faded on these vintage boots to more muted shades of red, white, and green. Made by Little's Boots.

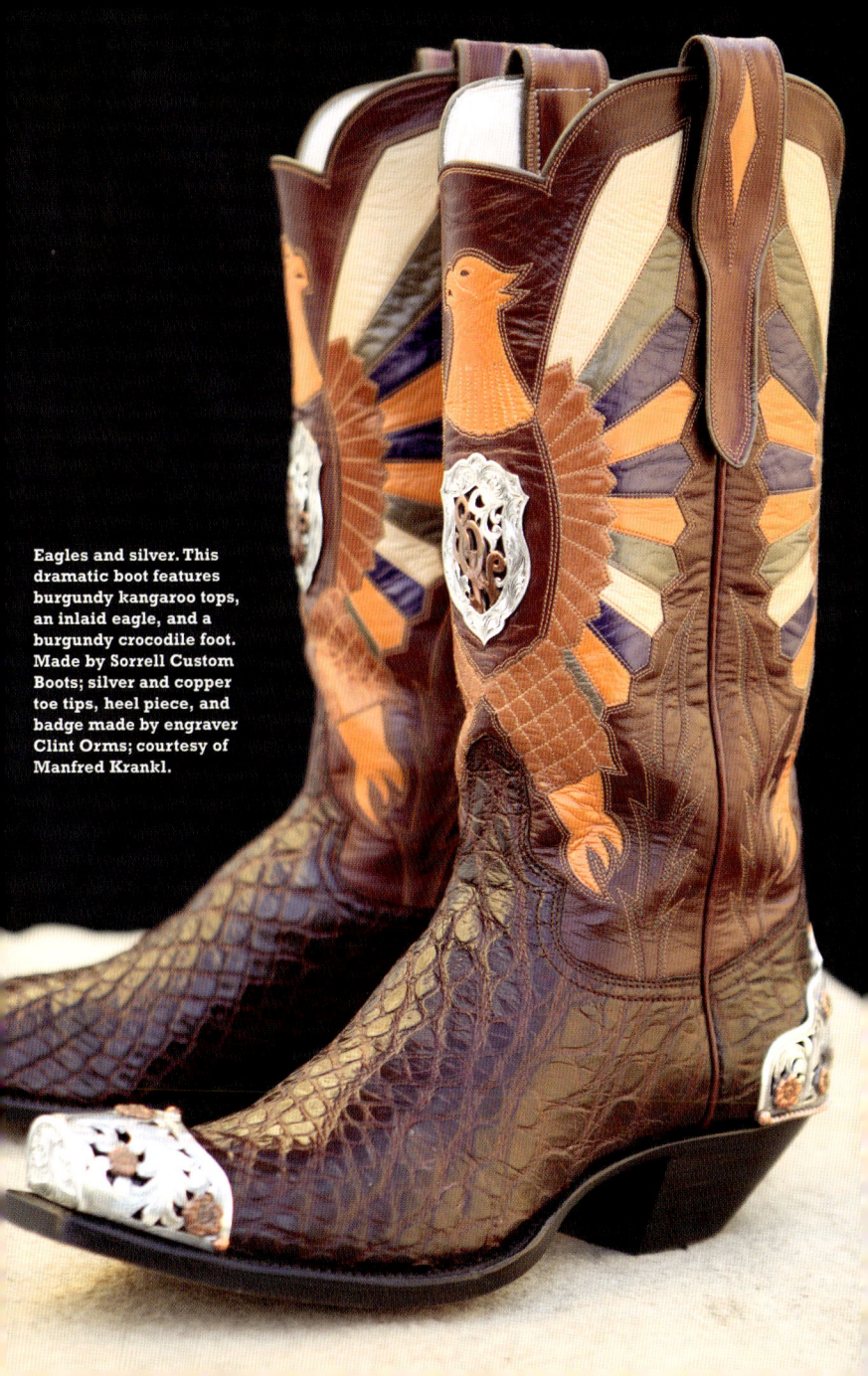

Eagles and silver. This dramatic boot features burgundy kangaroo tops, an inlaid eagle, and a burgundy crocodile foot. Made by Sorrell Custom Boots; silver and copper toe tips, heel piece, and badge made by engraver Clint Orms; courtesy of Manfred Krankl.

Newfound glory. A reproduction of late-1950s Hyer-made boots, this version stays true to the original and flies a flag with only forty-eight stars. Hyer Boot Company made several pairs of these boots to exhibit at rodeos, state fairs, and special store openings. Made by Sorrell Custom Boots; toe tips by Clint Orms; courtesy of Bruce Cole.

> Boots rarely feature eagles in profile or in "landing poses."

stars like Roy Rogers, who was remembered for his wide-winged eagle inlays in red, white, and blue.

Eagle boots come in all colors, although many of the early eagle boots were simply black and white. Eagles are an inherently macho design, allowing men the leeway to add three or more colors to a boot top without sacrificing any of the boot's manly impact. Many an eagle has been inlaid with a shield on its breast, or sometimes with a simple red heart.

There is no shortcut for stitching an inlaid boot top, but eagle designs were so popular that bootmakers would often use a machine press (or "clicker") and eagle-shaped metal dies (akin to large cookie cutters) to keep up with demand.

Stars and Stripes

There are men who would argue that red, white, and blue goes with every outfit, but it wasn't until the 1970s that wearing a flag was considered fashionable, or even acceptable. In 1968, radical Abbie Hoffman shocked the country and was jailed for wearing a button-down flag shirt. Two decades later, an identical shirt was worn by thousands of people attending Garth Brooks concerts nationwide.

The American flag was stitched on cowboy boots during the early 1950s, but the majority of these boots were "exhibition boots" meant to convey national pride and showcase the talent of American boot companies. The flag was stitched realistically, along with its flagpole—to do otherwise would have been viewed as vulgar commercialization.

Since then, flags have been interpreted in various ways on cowboy boots. Small exact replicas with stitching for all fifty stars is one extreme, while simple red and white striped boots with stars along the collar is another.

You can date certain vintage flag boots by counting the stars. The forty-eight-star flag flew until 1959, when Alaska was granted statehood. The flag reached its current fifty-star status in 1960, once Hawaii joined the union.

The American flag enjoyed a major revival in 1976. In celebration of America's bicentennial, the stars and stripes

1976 star. Made by Pablo Jass, Jass Boot Shop; courtesy of James Willett.

"Freedom Trail." Made by Rocketbuster Boots.

Six rows or more of stitching are often sewn on custom boots. An expert bootmaker will change thread colors, one row at a time, brightening the design as if adjusting a volume dial. Made by Dave J. Hutchings' Boots.

Constellation. Made by
Austin-Hall Boot Company;
courtesy of Wayne Learned.

were painted on countless consumer items and everyday objects. Everything was fair game, including our nation's fire hydrants.

"I always get a chill up and down my spine when I say the Pledge of Allegiance."
President Ronald Reagan, on Flag Day, June 14, 1985

The popularity of red, white, and blue cowboy boots took hold during the 1980s and the Reagan presidency. What was once thought of as "parade wear" was now looked upon as everyday patriotism.

Texas

"Texas is a state of mind, Texas is an obsession. Above all, Texas is a nation in every sense of the word."
John Steinbeck, *Travels with Charley*

Texas is America's second largest state, both in terms of population and geographical size. Although there has never been an official count, it is safe to say that more cowboy boots are made and worn in Texas than anywhere else in the country.

Today, there are close to two hundred custom bootmakers in Texas, more than the rest of the states combined. Historically, small one-man boot shops sprang up across Texas, one in each county. There is an unmatched joy and pride to making and owning a Texas boot, perhaps because a love of Texas is something deeply felt by customer and bootmaker alike.

The rich and abundant visual language used to identify and celebrate Texas includes stars, flags, flowers, landmarks like the Alamo, and the distinctive shape of the state itself.

Cowboy boots can spell "Texas" in many ways. A single or "lone" star has been a recognizable symbol of Texas since it was first stitched on a regional flag back in 1819. A five-pointed white star stitched on a boot denoted "Texas" at a

Motif and Metaphor

time when many cowboys could not read or write. Later, when geopolitical borders had been settled, boots were decorated with pieces of inlay or overlay cut in the distinctive Texas shape.

Graphically bold and thankfully short, the word "TEXAS" has been inlaid, tooled, and stitched into countless boot tops. Often those five letters wrap along the boot top at the collar, or along the sides on a mule ear boot pull, giving TEXAS top billing over all other decoration and imagery.

"You may all go to hell and I will go to Texas."
Davy Crockett, congressman and folk hero

The tricolor flag associated with the state first flew over the Republic of Texas from 1839 to 1845 when it was an independent nation. In 1845, it was adopted as the official flag when Texas became the twenty-eighth state. The meaning behind the flag's colors is the same as the American flag: blue for loyalty, white for strength, and red for bravery.

Local bootmakers Tex Robin and Duck Menzies are known for their creativity, enthusiasm, and the large number of Texas boots they have made for customers over the years. Duck has fit up to twelve Texas flags on a single pair by stitching them on the tops, around the collars, and on the pulls and vamps.

Since the 1980s, just about anything red, white, and blue goes, including morphing the Texas flag with other regional symbols like armadillos and chili peppers.

Texas boots. Made by Duck Menzies Bootmaker; courtesy of Bob Statzer.

Eagle tooled tops. Made by Jack Reed's Custom Made Boots; hand-carved by Ronald McIntire; courtesy of John Tongate.

Texas longhorn. Made by Charlie Dunn, Buck Steiner Maker; collection of John Tongate.

Big star. Made by Stephanie Ferguson Custom Boots.

Lone star. The flagpole provides a strong vertical line and contrast for the motion implied in the flag. Made by Back at the Ranch.

Mexican border boot, 1950s. Although intricate, this is a stock pattern. The colors and the name on the mule ears would change with each customer. Maker unknown; courtesy of Evan Voyles.

The Alamo changed hands at least sixteen times among Spanish, Mexican, Texan, Union, and Confederate forces. Today it is a cherished Texas symbol of heroism and the fight for freedom. Made by Sorrell Custom Boots; courtesy of Bruce Cole.

God bless Texas. Made by
Tres Outlaws.

State flag. Made by Tres Outlaws.

Texas state boot. Made by Lucchese Boot Company circa 1951.

"Sweetheart of the Rodeo." The silver toe caps are hand-tooled and painted. Made by Rocketbuster Boots.

Pretty Girls and Loose Women

Pretty girls have long been carved on the bows of ships and painted on the noses of warplanes. Today you can also see them inlaid and stitched onto cowboy boots.

Cowboy boots have an undeniable masculinity. And like a World War II barracks or a mechanic's garage, a man's boot top is usually not seen by the general public. This makes it a natural setting for pinup art. Women portrayed on cowboy boots are sexy, playful, and sometimes, downright rowdy.

Consumer demand is outpacing old-school bootmakers' willingness to stitch or tool these provocative designs. Younger bootmakers with urban upbringings are more inclined to take on these projects, viewing them as unique design challenges in the context of modern bootmaking.

Custom bootmakers Nevena Christi and Pascal are accomplished freehand artists, possessing a required skill set for this kind of figurative leather tooling. Pascal is also the only known bootmaker who also has firsthand experience as a tattooist.

There is no discernable difference between the designs of tooled cowboy boot tops and tattoo flash. Although they are rendered differently, the colors and artwork are interchangeable. Cowboy boots decorated with the female form have blurred the line between fashion and body art.

"Liberty Rock & Roll."
Made by Liberty Boot
Company.

"Lady Luck." Made by Rocketbuster Boots.

"Ride 'em Cowboy."
Made by Back at the
Ranch.

Nearly a calendar's worth of pinups are carved into these Rocketbuster boots.

Re-branding. TNN has now become Country Music Television (CMT). Made by Jim Babchak.

Individualism

The West has always been about being your own man (or woman). For some folks, boots inlaid with their own name, brand, or initials are the epitome of custom-made. In this day of logo- and label-driven fashion, custom cowboy boots distinguish themselves by celebrating their owner, not their maker.

Brands and Symbols

Cattle brands have been called "the heraldry of the range" and "cowboy hieroglyphics." Symbolic and beautiful, brands are usually made up of numbers, pictures, capital letters of the alphabet, and special characters like a slash, bar, or circle. Brands are read from top to bottom and left to right.

Most working ranches have a registered brand. For a rancher to put his full name on his truck, gate, or boots might seem vain. But according to Arnold Oren, a ranching historian and storyteller, "It is never conceit to display one's cattle brand." An old ranch brand is more than a personal trademark or mark of ownership. Each one represents a specific time, place, and legacy.

Some bootmakers will add a brand to a custom boot for as little as thirty five dollars. A creative bootmaker like Clay Hathaway can devise a suitable "brand-new" brand for a customer who doesn't already have one. (This author's own "Rocking Double J" is an example of a brand that represents a state of mind rather than a piece of dirt.)

Some cowboy boots are brainteasers, with owners' names such as "Robin" or "Rosie" depicted as rebuses or visual puns. Using pictures as stand-ins for names is actually a timeworn technique called canting, often found in medieval European heraldry.

Austin customer A. W. Finger had bootmaker Duck Menzies make several pairs of boots, each of which featured a carefully inlaid "single-finger salute," affectionately referred to as the "family crest."

"Miss Rodeo Oregon 2006." Made by Tres Outlaws; worn by Trena Loftesness of Sherwood, Oregon.

"Boss Lady." Made by Rocketbuster Boots.

"Robin's Boots." Made by Sorrell Custom Boots; courtesy of Robin Merrill.

Lazy H Ranch brand. Made by Brian Thomas Boots; courtesy of Richard Hasten.

Historic brands. Made by Little's Boots.

Brand loyalty. Made by Rocketbuster Boots; worn by photographer Marty Snortum.

Rocking W brand. Made by C. T. Boot Shop; courtesy of James Willett.

Rafter Double B brand.
Made by Jim Covington;
courtesy of Mark
Bukowski.

Baby blue ostrich. Cowboy Boots by George; collection of Alexis Millward.

A. W. Finger boots. Made by
Duck Menzies Bootmaker;
courtesy of Mark Fletcher.

Many of the historic Texas brands come with a story (even if it's not true). The origin of the "6666" brand is unknown, but many have come to believe it commemorates the poker hand that won the land surrounding the town of Guthrie. Likewise, the XIT brand, originally designed to thwart rustlers, is instead remembered to this day as "10 in Texas," a ranch so large it covered portions of ten Texas counties.

Initials and Names

Initials can be found almost anywhere on a boot: front and center, on the collar, on the pulls, or near the wearer's ankle. Stand-alone initials naturally fill a boot top, making them some of the most versatile yet meaningful design elements.

Charlie Dunn is remembered for his elegant cursive writing, an inlaid leather signature that usually included the wearer's entire first and last names. Mirrored along the boots' side seam, the letters trailed off into the stitching. The designs were almost ethereal.

Mule ears, popular on cowboy boots throughout the 1950s, often featured names running vertically, similar to a county fair prize ribbon.

Trophy boots memorialize events and celebrate accomplishments, such as winning a competition or holding political office. Many have a brash, showy feel, but isn't that precisely the point?

PAGE 253 *top:* **Signature boots. Made by Lee Miller, Texas Traditions; courtesy of John Tongate.** *bottom:* **"Jessel." Boot tops made by Little's Boots.**

Motif and Metaphor

Fit for a rodeo queen. Vintage eagle boots are uncommon for women. Although they can be found in small sizes, eagle boots were made for men and young boys. Instead, women tended to wear butterflies. Collection of Karen Robinson.

Tiger swallowtail. Made by Kimmel Boots; courtesy of Evan Voyles.

Austin·Texas

John Tongate

JESSE

Wild python. Made by Melody's Custom Boots; courtesy of Deana McGuffin.

"WD." Made by Duck Menzies Bootmaker; courtesy of Wayne Duncan.

Mirror writing. Made by Charlie Dunn, Texas Traditions; courtesy of Lee and Carrlyn Miller.

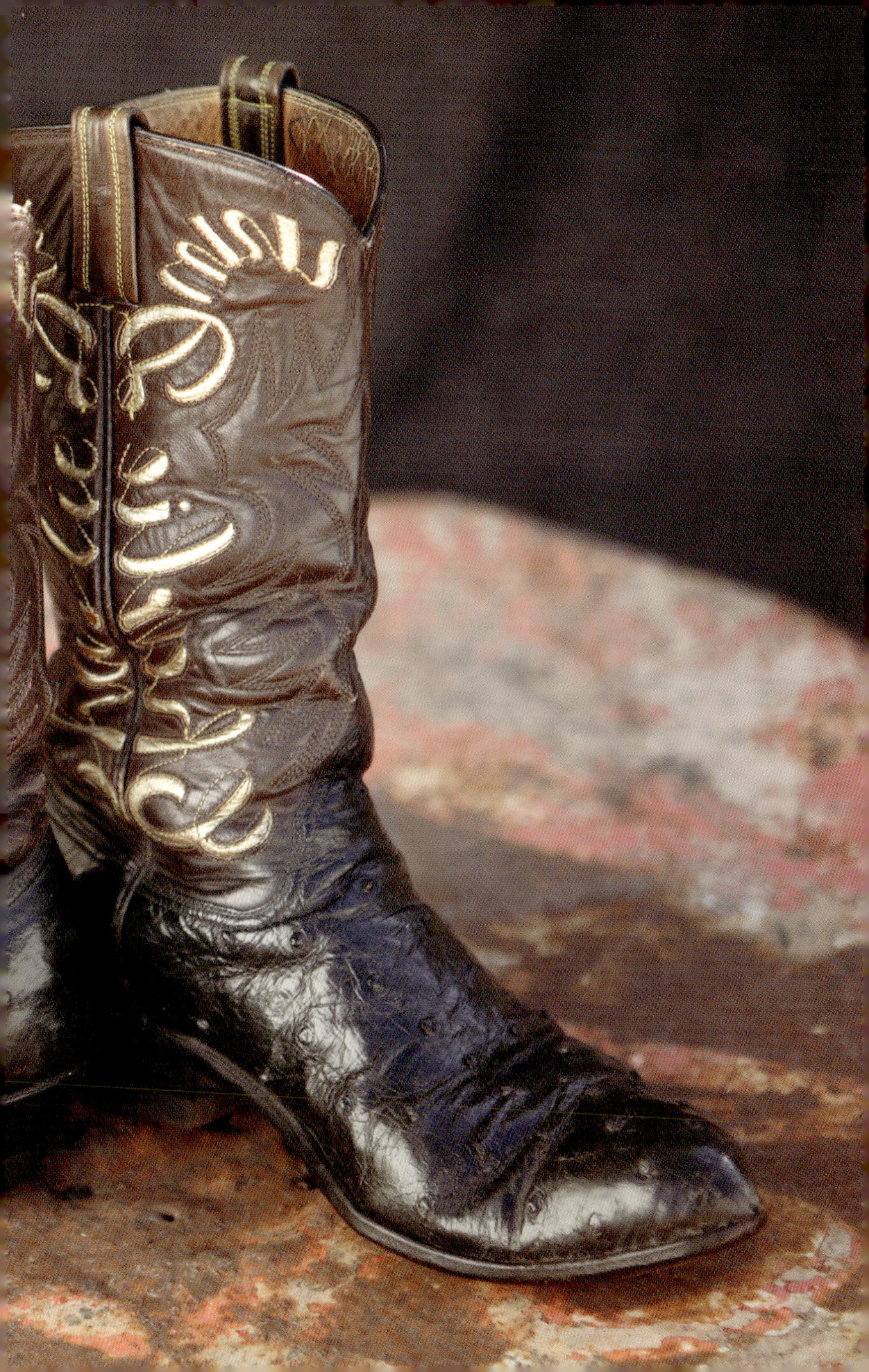

Tooled mule ears. Made by Riff Raff Leatherworks; carving by Carey Blanchard; courtesy of Jeff Borins.

"Bigon" eagles. Made by Ramirez & Sons Boot Manufacturing; courtesy of Cliff McCall.

The overlay shapes stay the same, and the burgundy and Benedictine colors are flipped and echoed. Initials pop. Made by Kimmel Boots; worn by Teresa Beard; courtesy of Tyler Beard.

Home on the range. Made by Slickfork Boots; courtesy of Chris A. Lucker.

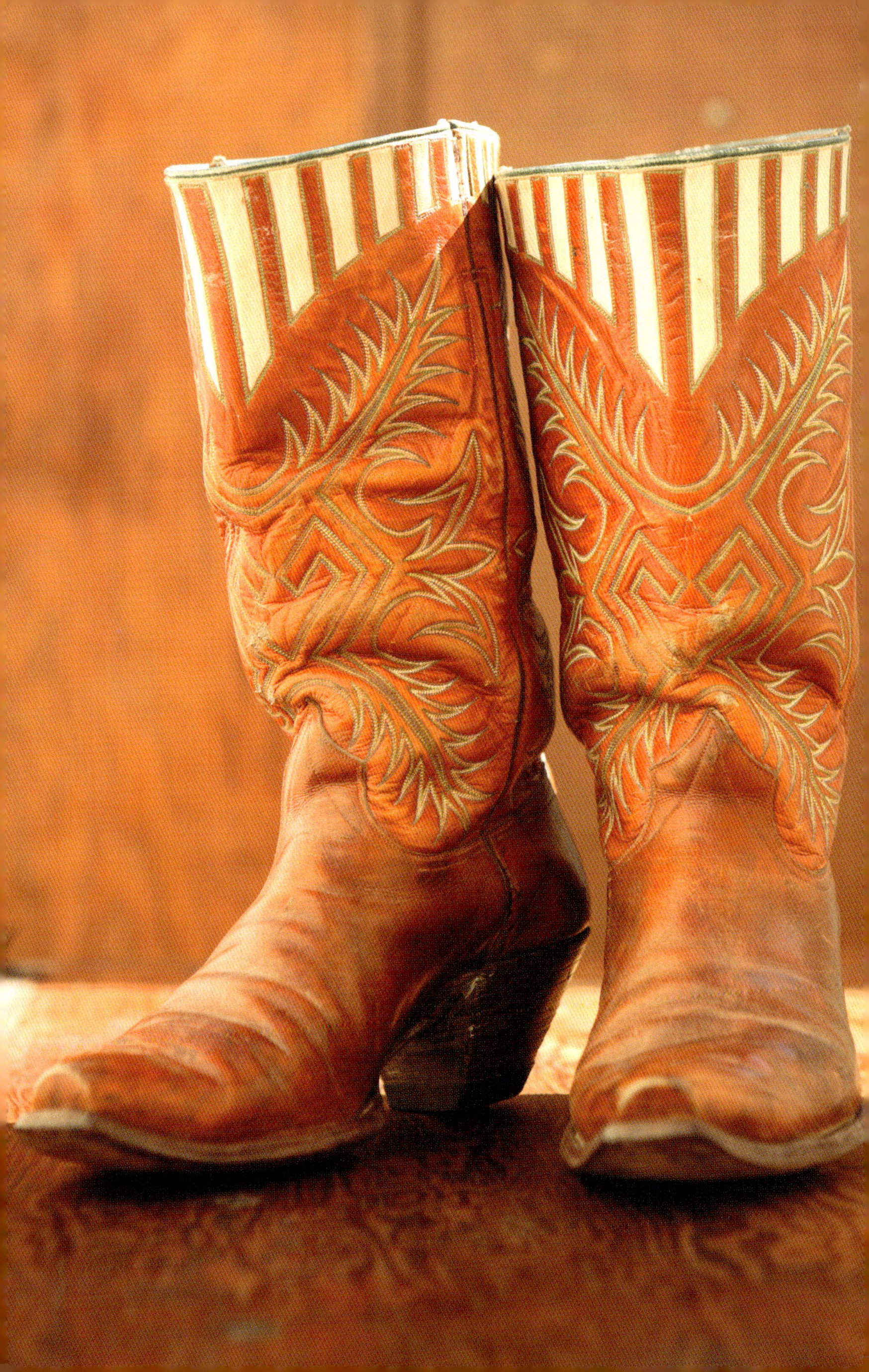

VINTAGE COWBOY BOOTS

Yellow burst. Made by Stewart Romero; courtesy of D. Alan Calhoun.

Vintage cowboy boots remain highly prized objects of western Americana. Many pairs continue to be worn, while others are valued as purely decorative items.

Vintage boots are becoming increasingly hard to find—especially those made during the "golden days of inlay" in the late 1940s. Today, the price of a vintage boot depends on its style, condition, and rarity.

Impressive "top shelf" vintage collections include outstanding design work and hard-to-find maker's labels.

Older custom-made boots can be difficult to come by because they are fewer in number than factory boots, and because they tend to be highly personal items, frequently remaining within families for generations. Many custom pairs are unsigned and have no label to identify the bootmaker. In such cases, collectors look for signature stitchwork, pull straps, or tongue patterns for clues and guidance.

In some instances, works by well-known and prolific bootmakers like Ray Jones and Paul Bond are unusual finds on the vintage market. These and similar makers build boots for hardworking cowboys and ranchers, and the boots rarely survive in good enough condition to be sold a second time.

Boot companies like Olsen-Stelzer, Hyer, and M. L. Leddy's have all enjoyed successful catalog business, which helps to provide name recognition and prestige to their vintage pairs. Their print catalogs are prized collectors' items in their own right, desirable for their artwork and usefulness in identifying and dating designs.

Collectors who enjoy a real challenge search for boots in their size only. There's an odd sense of destiny when you find a boot that fits, as if you're continuing an adventure that has already begun.

The frustrating truth is that vintage boots are difficult if not impossible to find in large sizes. Back in 1920, Justin Boots ranged from sizes four to nine, and sizes eight and nine were uncommonly large. Today, the average American man wears a size ten and a half shoe. Vintage cowboy boots appearing

PAGE 262
This vintage pair offers the illusion of a scallop boot top. Maker unknown; courtesy of Mike Hathorn.

in today's estate sales are most often size nine, an uncomfortable lag behind contemporary sizes.

Women fare much better because they can get rough-and-tumble style by wearing the smaller men's sizes. Larry Jennings, owner of the shop Cowboy Legends, in Santa Fe, New Mexico, which is considered a clearinghouse for vintage boots, says that women now make up 85 percent of his customers. Boot brands like Acme, Corral, Texas, and Gold Bond are in high demand for their retro-style and "cloth pulls." Jennings adds that women are drawn to the box toe, colorful inlay, and easy fit afforded by the extra-short tops.

Men seek out vintage boots in larger sizes and wearable condition, such as the Tony Lama "black label" boots of the 1970s and 1980s. Despite their age, these boots routinely sell for more than their contemporary counterparts because of their superior quality in both materials and craftsmanship, as evidenced by the pegged shanks and the noticeable heft of the leather soles.

If you are buying vintage boots with the intention of wearing them, you should consider the age of the materials, realizing that a less-than-perfect fit will be harder on the boot than the wearer. Dried-out leather cracks and tears easily and will not survive the stresses of resoling or other repairs. So enjoy your boots while they last.

Cloth pull. Made by Olsen-Stelzer Boot Company; courtesy of Laura Neitzel.

The most beautiful western boots ever created!
Golden
ANGUS
ACME BOOTS
A magnificent "Steerhead" design . . . richly inlaid with golden leathers! Intricate multi-color stitching! Eye-catching underlays!
The Golden Angus is Acme's finest . . . the most beautiful of all western boots—ever! Many colors and combinations! Many styles of heels and toes! Your Acme dealer will be glad to show you!
Design patent applied for.
Mens Style No. 4850
Boys and Girls Style No. 2213
WORLD'S LARGEST BOOTMAKERS
They cost less than you think!
Mens . . . . .from $16.95
Boys and Girls . . . . .from $5.95 - $10.95, according to size
Boys and Girls Style No. 2209
Acme Boots are worn by stars and featured players of Warner Bros. western television and motion picture productions.
Clint Walker stars in "CHEYENNE"
Will Hutchins stars in "SUGARFOOT"
Jack Kelly and James Garner star in "MAVERICK"
Boys and Girls Style No. 2760
Boys and Girls Style No. 2722
Boys and Girls Style No. 2743
Ask your dealer for an Acme Gift Certificate!
ACME BOOTS A Gift...
Acme Boot Company, Inc., Clarksville, Tennessee
SUBSIDIARY OF PHILADELPHIA AND READING CORPORATION

Finding Vintage Boots

- Although vintage cowboy boots can still be found throughout the American Southwest in antique stores, flea markets, and yard sales, a small group of experienced dealers and eBay offer the most dependable selection to choose from.

- Located on an age-old trade route, Santa Fe, New Mexico, has more vintage boots than anyplace else. Worn boots are bought, sold, and traded back and forth. It's a great place to collect stories as well as boots.

- The Internet is an invaluable tool for serious boot collectors. Using well-crafted keyword searches, boot enthusiasts can target their collecting by era, maker, or even size.

- The feverish selling and buying on eBay has become something of a spectator sport, providing a community of computer-savvy collectors with the chance to share information about and admiration for one-of-a-kind boots.

Remaking Vintage Patterns

Many collectors look for vintage boots that appeal to them, regardless of fit or condition, and have them remade in their size by custom makers.

While bootmakers consider it bad manners to copy a boot made by a colleague still in business, many shops are willing to adapt or reproduce classic vintage pairs and those attributed to "maker unknown."

Lisa Sorrell is a skilled bootmaker who enjoys the challenge of reproducing old designs. Oftentimes Sorrell is handed a photo of a vintage boot and she must improvise the unseen portions of it. Rather than using her favorite artwork, she tries to honor the original maker and anticipate what his or her design choices might have been. In a sense, she creates tributes rather than straight copies.

Acme Boots produced some great inlay patterns, including the "Golden Angus." Occasionally these mass-produced designs are remade by top custom boot shops like Dave Little's Boots. In such cases, the quality of the materials and craftsmanship far surpasses that found in the factory-made original.

OPPOSITE
Golden Angus by Acme Boots circa 1960. Some vintage boots are remade using catalog illustrations or magazine ads like this one. Collection of Jennifer June.

Golden angus. An Acme Boot design remade by Little's Boots; courtesy of John Tongate.

When reproducing vintage boots, matching the colors can be difficult. Leather colors come and go with fashion, and original colors can fade to unintended shades. To capture a vintage look, try using softer colors, and a tone-on-tone color difference between the top and the vamp. Choose bone-colored leathers over a bright white.

Whether it's a longer or rounder toe, taller top, or larger calf measurement, a vintage boot reproduced in a bigger size presents unique design challenges. Leaving too much space between elements, like inlay shapes, can weaken a design. As a vintage boot is rescaled for a larger reproduction boot, care is needed to preserve the design's energy.

Certain designs are meant to be big and bold. Our eyes use shape to recognize objects and grasp their meaning. For instance, the detailed silhouette of a bucking bronco should be nearly as large on a boot as it is on a Wyoming license plate; otherwise it loses its punch.

Try boot tops crowded with small inlay, or plain tops with simple bold shapes. Don't settle for a compromise: the impact lies in the extremes.

This boot top from the 1950s has it all—inlay, overlay, fancy stitching, and hand lacing. Made by **Abraham Rios**; courtesy of **Evan Voyles**.

A vintage bluebird boot—good as new. Made by Lee Miller, Texas Traditions; topstitching by Julia Parmentor.

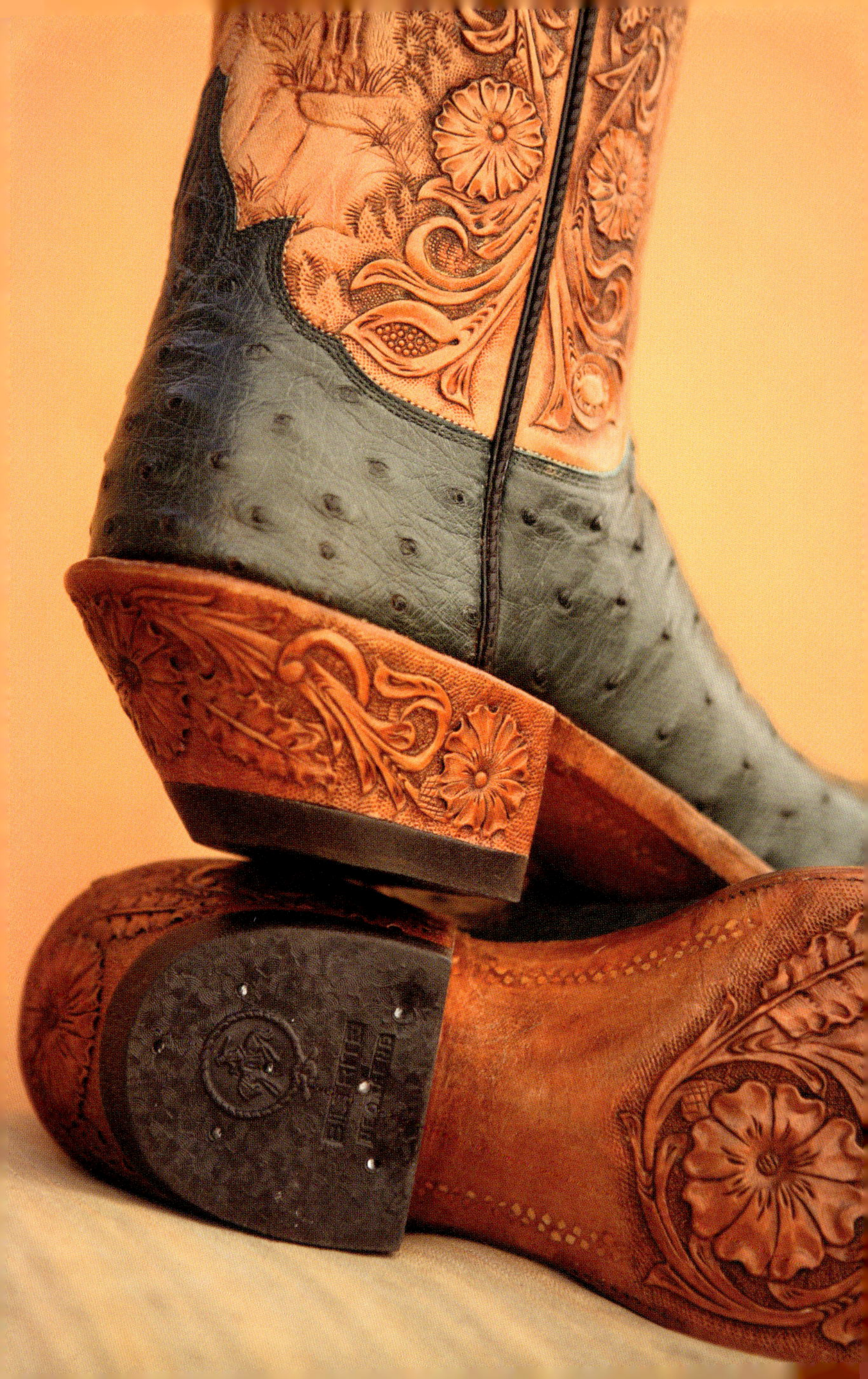

SOLE SEARCHIN': BUILDING A BOOT

Children's boots with simple cutouts and plastic soles. Factory-made; courtesy of Mike Hathorn.

Ask any bootmaker and he or she will tell you it doesn't matter what's stitched on a boot top—rhinestones or dancing girls—the first thing customers do is turn a boot over and stare at its sole. What are they looking for?

With cowboy boots, you'll find building techniques and materials used in no other footwear. This chapter outlines what makes a cowboy boot truly unique; it's not the decoration, but rather the materials, fit, and style.

Measurement and Fit

How your cowboy boots fit is very important. With a good fit, cowboy boots look better, feel better, and last longer.

Cowboy boots must fit your foot without the help of laces. The key to a well-fitting cowboy boot is a snug fit around the top of your foot. This keeps your foot from sliding forward and jamming your toes, while giving you the full benefit of the boot's arch support.

Longtime bootmaker Sam Lucchese believed a human foot could feel a $1/16$-inch circumference difference in the tightness or looseness of a boot. Custom bootmakers take at least six measurements of each foot. Many measurements are taken twice—once with customers seated and legs crossed, and again with customers standing so their feet are bearing their full weight.

It is natural for a person's foot measurements and boot size to change over time. Everything from a weight gain of fifteen pounds to a pregnancy or driving a car with a manual transmission can change how well a cowboy boot fits.

"If they don't fit, they aren't worth a darn."
Charlie Dunn, bootmaker

PAGE 274
Vanishing art. The heels and soles of the boots have been hand-carved. Made by C. T. Boot Shop.

Lastmaking

A custom bootmaker will take a customer's measurements and use them to shape a last. A last is a wooden or plastic form. Rather than being a model of the foot, the last captures the cowboy boot's interior space, incorporating both the foot width and diameter, and also the toe shape and heel height.

Boot lasts come in standard sizes and are then either built up with pieces of leather or ground away in order to match a customer's individual measurements. Sometimes bootmakers will spend more time setting up a last than making the boot. Once a good fit is achieved, most bootmakers save a customer's last for the next time he or she places an order.

A cowboy boot is built and shaped around the last. Damp leather is pulled and tacked down. The boot dries and its sole is pegged while on the last. The last is then pulled out, and the pegs left poking up through the insole are sanded down only at the very end.

Tools

All the early bootmaking tools were hand tools: hammers, pliers, awls, and knives. In order to save the bootmaker time picking up and putting down tools, special hand tools like lasting pliers evolved. Lasting pliers are curved pliers with a small hammerhead attached underneath. The bootmaker uses lasting pliers to pull the leather across the last and then tack it down in place. Since the pliers and hammer are combined into a single tool, lasting a boot goes much more quickly, with only a slight change of grip on the tool.

Little has changed with most of the tools used to make boots. There is a smooth hammer to help flatten and shape the leather; a short-handled hammer with a broad texture head to hammer in wooden pegs. There are two kinds of awls: one to punch pilot holes for the pegging, since unlike nails, pegs would snap and break; and another awl to punch holes through the insole, so the inseaming thread can be laced and pulled tight.

PAGE 281 *top:* Worn heels. Maker unknown; courtesy of Evan Voyles. *bottom:* Boots made and signed by Charlie Dunn; courtesy of Evan Voyles.

Sole Searchin': Building a Boot

Originally, all the sole leather and stacked heels were shaped by hand using knives and files. Early on, hand-crank bench tools were developed to cut through the thick hides. These cutters are still used by shoemakers and bootmakers alike, but electricity is now used to power sewing machines and the spinning brushes and abrasive drums used to shape and finish the sole.

Quality

A quality boot will stand up straight without the help of boot trees or other supports. The left and right boot will look like a perfect pair, with the tops, toes, and heels matching each other. The seams will line up. The stitches will closely follow the skived edges of the leather. The inlays will lie flat. The heel and sole will be neatly inked and polished to a shine.

A straight top and a polished look are signs of a quality boot. Made by Daly Boots.

Charlie Dunn
1-187

Cut, carved, and painted vamp. Made by Rocketbuster Boots.

Steps to Making a Cowboy Boot

1. *Measuring*
   Take foot and calf measurements.

2. *Design*
   Select leather.
   Choose toe and heel style.
   Design boot tops.

3. *Boot Tops*
   Prepare paper patterns.
   Cut tops, lining, and pull straps out of leather.
   Thin ("skive") edges of pieces.
   Assemble tops with cement, including piping.
   Sew tops with inlays, overlays, and stitch patterns.

4. *Vamps*
   Cut vamps and lining pieces.
   Stretch wet vamps and linings over crimpboards.
   Allow to dry thoroughly.
   Measure, trim, and attach vamps to boot tops.

5. *Heel Counters*
   Cut out hard leather counter and counter cover.
   Attach heel counter to boot top and skive edges.
   Sew counter and counter cover to top. Trim.

6. *Side Seaming and Pull Straps*
   Cut, cement, and sew side welt ("piping").
   Rub seams down flat.
   Attach pull straps.
   Turn tops right-side out.

7. *Fitting the Last*
   Compare standard last to foot measurements.
   Build up last with leather (if necessary).
   Smooth finish.

8. *Insole*
   Nail insole to last.
   Trim and shape insole.

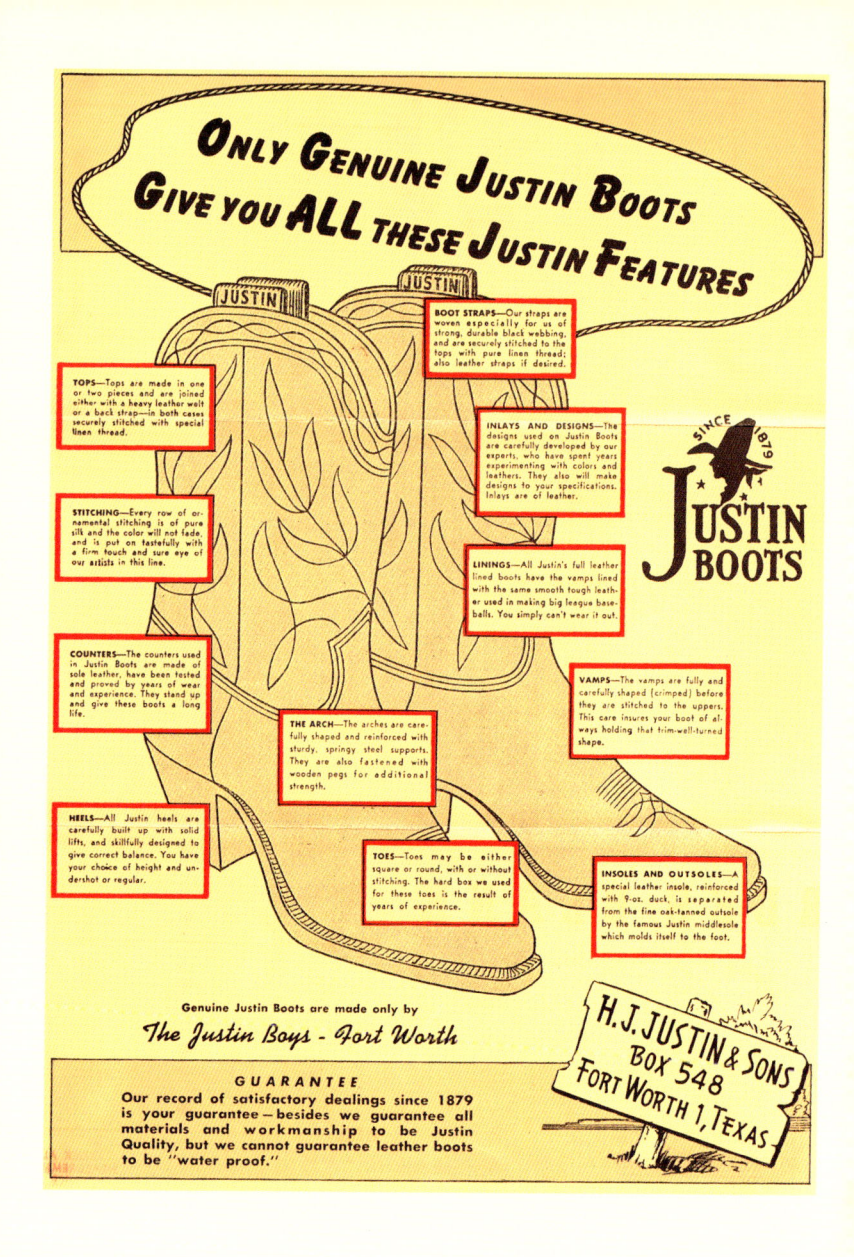

Boot features. Sales
brochure for Justin Boots;
collection of Jennifer June.

9. *Lasting*
    Stretch wet vamp and counter over last.
    Anchor with tacks and allow to dry.
    Turn back vamp leather and position toe boxes.
    Cement, dry, and smooth toe boxes.
    Pull and re-tack vamp leather over toe boxes.

10. *Inseaming*
    Punch holes through insole with awl.
    Stitch inseaming thread through welt and insole.
    Trim and flatten seam.
    Sew in shank or flattened 40-penny nail.
    Peg around heel.
    Fill in shank and bottom of insole with leather pieces.
    Shape or grind shank and then peg.

11. *Attaching Soles and Pegging*
    Trim welt to desired width.
    Cement and trim sole to welt.
    Sew and peg soles.
    Ink and finish front of soles.

12. *Stacking Heels*
    Stack, cement, and trim layers of heel leather.
    Nail or peg heels, and add rubber heel cap.
    Sand heels to final matching shape.

13. *Finishing*
    Ink and polish the heel.
    Pull the last out and sand down pegs inside boot.
    Insert heel pad.
    Wear and enjoy!

The Hide

Life on the open range can be hard on a steer hide. Bootmakers carefully avoid scars and brand marks, but planning how best to use a particular hide can be tricky.

Bootmakers prefer to cut certain boot pieces from special parts of the hide. This is easier to understand if you think of the "cow" in cowboy boot. The animal skin has greater stretch around its belly than it does running head-to-tail along its backbone.

The vamp (or foot) of the boot is always cut at a sharp 90-degree angle to the backbone of the hide. This means the stretch will run from heel to toe on the boot, and the foot of the boot will not "walk out of shape." The vamps get the prime real estate on a hide since these pieces bear the brunt of the wear, tear, and flexing.

The tops and pull straps are turned and cut along the backbone, so that the natural stretch of the leather runs around the leg, not up and down. This provides a helpful resistance as the wearer puts on the boots and pulls up on the tops. Even after years of use, well-made boot tops should not stretch out of shape.

Hair-on vamps and pulls.
Made by Kimmel Boots;
courtesy of Bryce Sunderlin.

Pascal's lightning-bolt maker's mark can always be found inked on the sole. Made by Riff Raff Leatherworks; courtesy of Lemmy Kilmister.

Soles

Historically, sole leather has been vegetable tanned (aged in pits piled with oak bark and other material rich in tannic acids). Before being inked or finished, tanned leather is a pale to reddish brown.

Stiff and durable like saddle leather, sole leather makes up the bottom portions of a cowboy boot: outer and inner soles, welt and heel. This leather is so dense and hard that, stacked for a heel, it's sometimes mistaken for wood.

Sole leather is rolled or hammered to flatten and compress the leather, making it more durable. The heels are stacked layer upon layer and held together with glue and pegs. On average, a $1^5/_8$-inch-high heel consists of five to ten layers of leather, hand placed, glued, and shaped by the bootmaker. The sole leather is shaped with a knife and nowadays smoothed with a drum or belt sander. The art is in the symmetry: each boot should be the mirror image of the other.

Nothing wears out fast on a cowboy boot. You might break a pull strap, but that's likely to be the only surprise; you'll see everything else coming a mile away. A worn-out sole may start as a small crack or a spot of wear that slowly wears through the outer sole. Not until the hole starts working its way through the inner sole will folks remove a boot long enough to get it repaired. This is the true function of the cowboy boot: endurance and flat-out dependability.

Arch

The curved and rounded arch gives a cowboy boot its distinctive look. Unlike most other kinds of footwear, the arch of a cowboy boot can take a real beating: on horseback, a stirrup rubs, dents, and mars the "working part of the cowboy boot." Grit and dirt act like sandpaper, adding to the wear and tear. A working cowboy is also exposed to muck and piss, known in polite company as "barn acids."

Traditionally the arch of a cowboy boot was formed and strengthened with a 40-penny nail, flattened using a sledge hammer and anvil. Now premade metal shanks are widely

Inked and burnished soles. Made by Brian Thomas Boots; courtesy of Richard Hasten.

Single row of pegs. Made by Vintage Kirkendall Boots; courtesy of Wayne Learned.

available, but many still use 40-penny nails as a nod to tradition. For others, a store-bought shank is a waste of money. The nail or shank is fastened tightly into the arch of the boot and covered with strips of leather.

Pegs

The sewn welt of a cowboy boot ends just behind the ball of the wearer's foot. The rest of the sole along the shank or arch of the boot is attached firmly with wood pegs. Tacks are used to hold the leather in place while the boot is drying or being inseamed, but a custom bootmaker removes them before the boot is finished.

Turn a boot over and you'll find two rows of wooden pegs; one row along each side of the shank (arch) of the boot. The beauty of the wooden peg is that it absorbs moisture and swells along with the boot's leather sole when it gets wet. The pegs are inked to match the color of the sole, but on a worn boot you can run your finger along a boot's arch and feel the bumps of slightly raised square wooden pegs.

Today's glues are strong enough to outlast any leather or stitch, so the pegs aren't as vital to the function of a cowboy boot as they once were. When you see a row of wooden pegs on a new pair of boots, they are a marker of tradition, craftsmanship, and skill.

For every peg on a boot's sole, a sharp awl is dipped in wax, a hole is punched, and a peg is hammered in. Bootmakers have a special hammer, with a textured face to grip the peg, and the hammer is set into a rhythmic motion: one light tap to set the peg in place, then a harder one to drive it in . . . over and over. The remarkable thing is that the hole punched with the bootmaker's awl is round and significantly smaller than the peg, contradicting the commonsense rule that you can't fit a square peg in a round hole.

Most "pegged" factory-made boots are now using rectangular peg-shaped brass nails instead of the traditional wooden pegs. Large boot companies prefer brass nails because they are fast and foolproof. If they can make a boot faster, it's

PAGE 294
top left: **"Starfire," Rocketbuster Boots.**
top right: **Creamsicle filigree, McGuffin Custom Boots.**
bottom right: **Round toes with red-stitched toe-bug and colored storm welt. Duck Menzies Bootmaker; courtesy of Wayne Duncan.**
bottom left: **Black-on-black wingtips. Made by Stewart Romero; courtesy of Mark Fletcher.**

Sole Searchin': Building a Boot

the same as making it cheaper. Manufacturers have kept the square shape, rather than using a round brass nail, out of respect for tradition and because customers have learned to turn a boot over and look for the pegs as a sign of boot quality.

Toes

Boot experts like Tyler Beard find little truth in the story that the pointed toe was invented to help a riding cowboy locate his saddle stirrup. Round or wide, square toes are the practical choice for working cowboy boots.

Toe styles come and go. Cowboy boots' macho appeal is due in part to the imagined discomfort of their pointed toes. What folks don't know is that these pointy toes are like Hollywood westerns: all fake fronts and swinging saloon doors. The wearer's toes are, in fact, sitting back at a comfortable distance. The shape of the tip of any boot toe is strictly a question of style and will not affect or compromise the fit.

More skill is required to make a pointed or box toe than a round one. Boot toes are strengthened with a toe box made from a stiff piece of either leather or celastic (fabric impregnated with plastic). Individually hand molded and shaped for the boot's toe style, the toe box fits between the lining and top leathers and is invisible to the wearer. Matching the right and left toes is no easy job, and the longer and narrower the toe box, the more difficult the task.

Toe styles change over time, usually every twenty to twenty-five years—effectively skipping a generation. This means that hand-me-down boots from a wearer's father might be cherished but will be viewed as old-fashioned . . . and will likely remain completely unworn. On the other hand, this same wearer will take his grandfather's boots to a custom shop and have replicas made in his size.

When you order custom boots, you get your choice of toe styles. Letters like u, h, j, and r are commonly used to describe rounded toe styles, but their precise meanings can vary from shop to shop, so customers should confirm their choice with their custom maker. Box toes are always measured horizontally

PAGE 295
top: **Custom wingtip. Made by Tres Outlaws.**
bottom: **Crocodile boots. Made by Sorrell Custom Boots; silver and copper toe tips by engraver Clint Orms; courtesy of Manfred Krankl.**

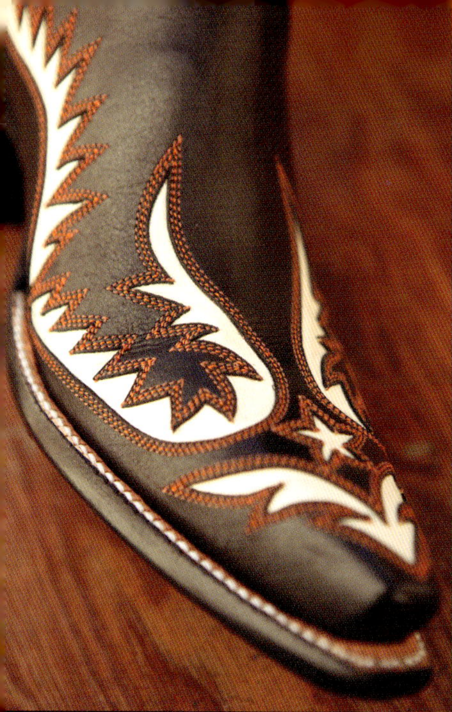
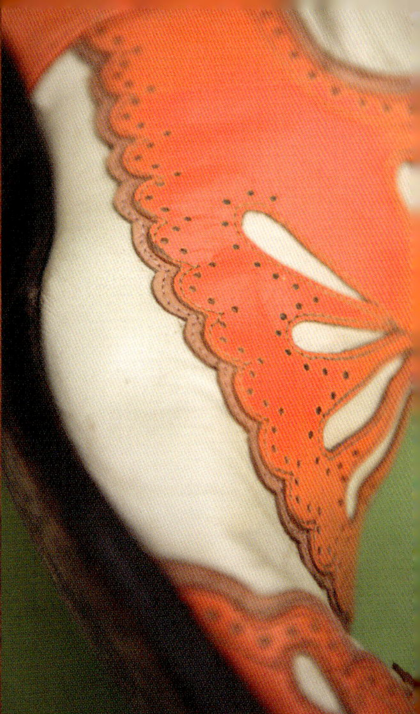
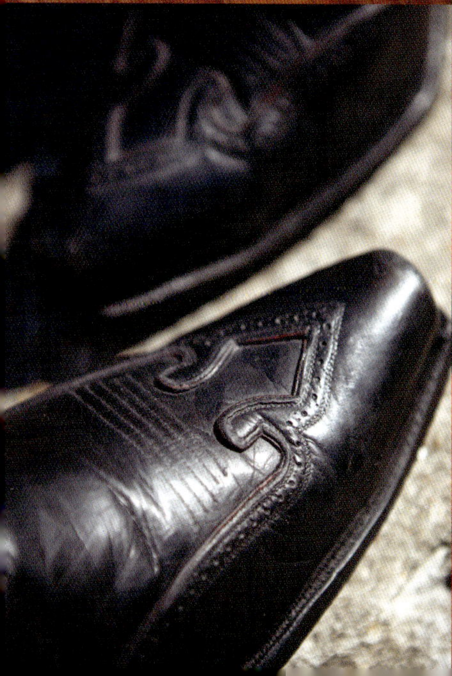
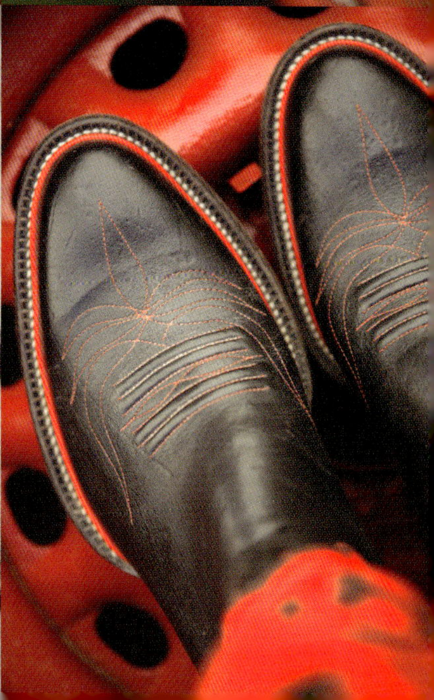

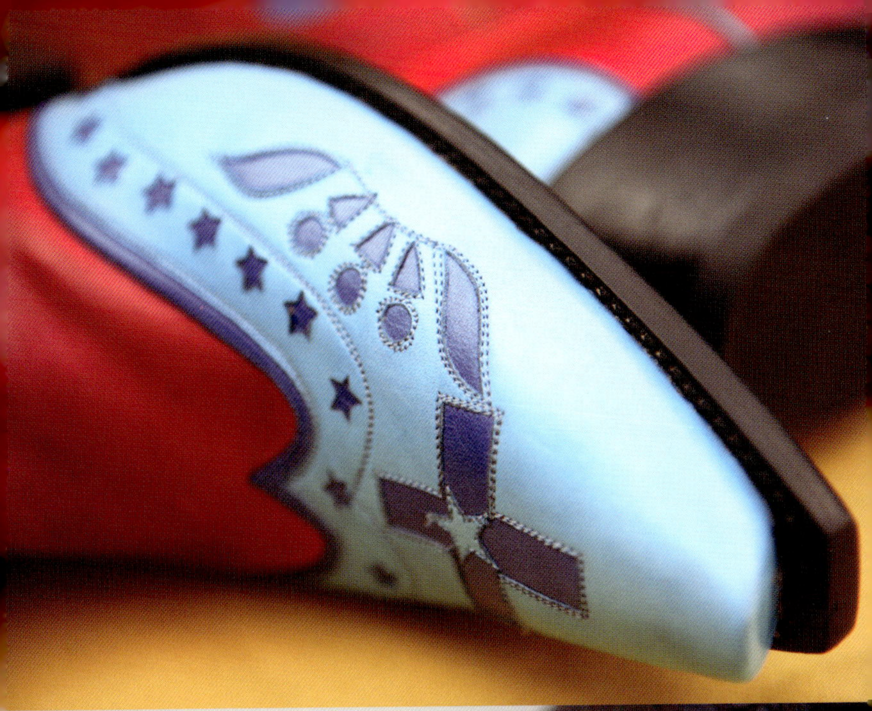
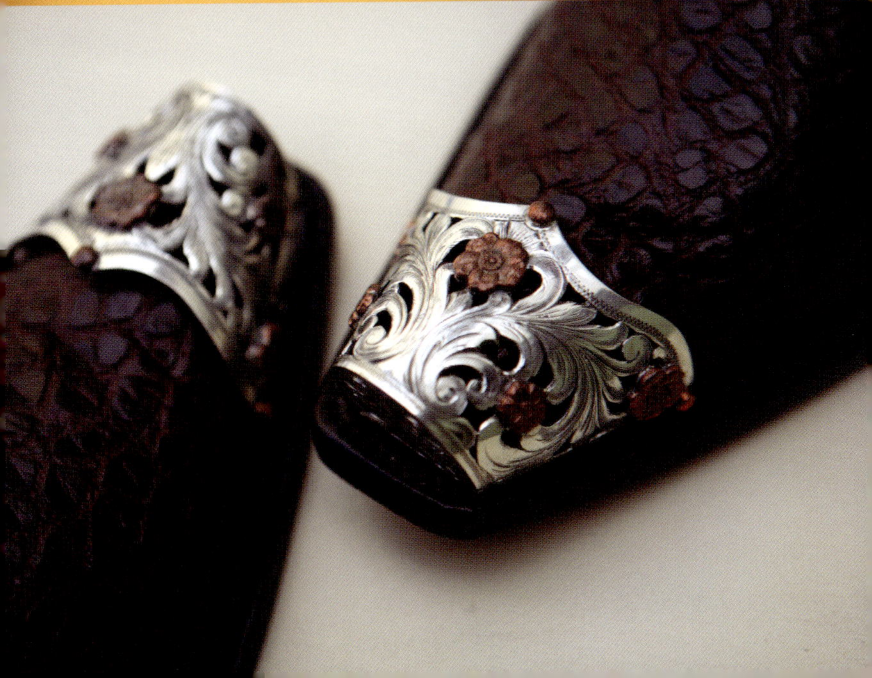

Lizard-skin toes on dress boots. Made by Lucchese Boot Company.

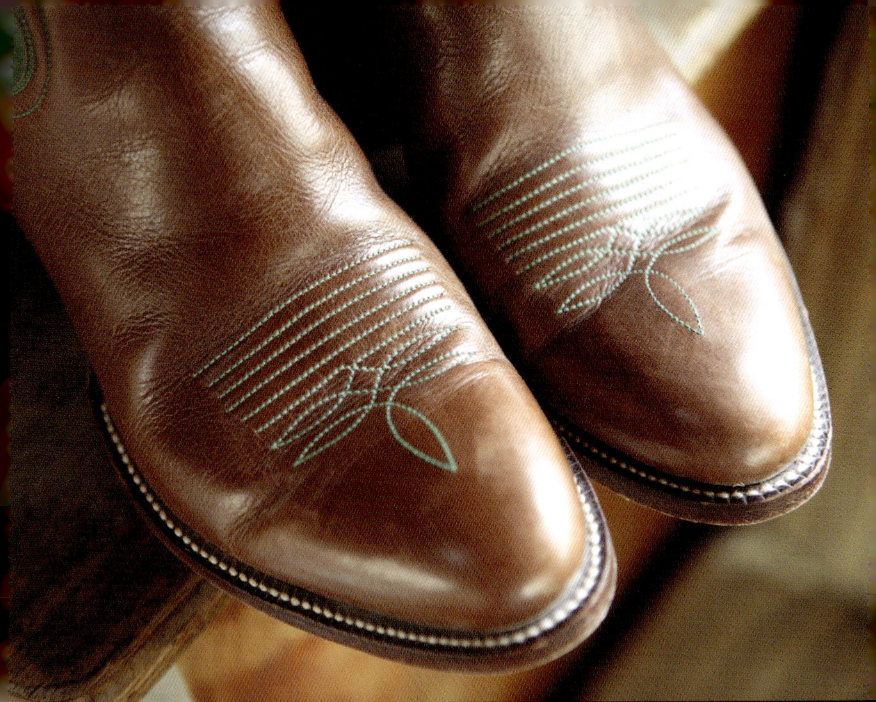
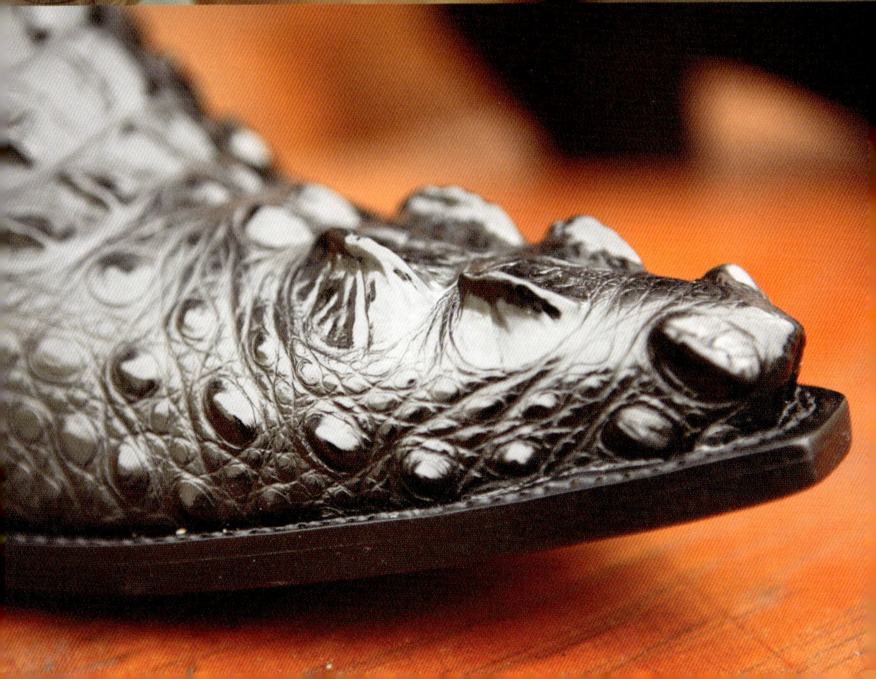

For some men, "cowboy" is a verb, not a noun—riding and roping (and frequent resoling). Made by Jim Covington; worn by Mark Bukowski.

at the boot tip: $1/4$ inch, $1/2$ inch, $3/4$ inch, and so on.

One toe that is very popular with the "dress boots and boardroom" crowd is a French- or Lucchese-style toe. It is a broad, slightly squared toe which slopes down toward the sole at the front of the boot. When paired with a low "walking" heel, these toes can fly successfully under the radar of even the most rigid corporate dress codes.

A boot's toe is sometimes the only feature shown off by its owner, so its shape, color, and fit are important fashion statements. Exotic hides are often used to dress up a boot, and wingtips and overlays of contrasting leathers (known as "foxing") can signal to others that the boot is something special.

Heels

It's true that a higher heel can help a cowboy grip the stirrup, but that's important only to a point. What's more important is that high heels give cowboys better arch support—and a confident swagger when they're walking across a barroom floor.

Heels reflect fashion and personal style more than function. An underslung (or "undershot") heel is one where the back of the heel angles forward as it descends to the ground, rather than running straight up and down. "Roper"-style boots have low "walking" heels, but most cowboy boots are made with underslung heels. The style and fashion depend on the degree of the angle. Tony Benattar launched his bootmaking career in 1987 with a high-styled pointy-toed line of cowboy boots. His early orders came mostly from musicians. According to Tony, "Those boots were so underslung, it was hard to step on your cigarette butt."

Cowboy boots are often the only "high heels" worn by men. To achieve the right look, pants should be worn a little longer, so the cuffs of the jeans dip below the top of the boot heels. The high heels and longer Levi's make the wearer look taller and the legs longer. Gaining an inch or two of height can give someone a whole new outlook. Which is sexier, a taller stance or increased confidence? Who knows, but does it really matter?

PAGE 297
top: Simple round toes are among the most popular. Made by Jim Covington; courtesy of Joanie McGrath.
bottom: Crocodile hornback. Made by Tres Outlaws.

Shark foot and collar with eight rows of stitching. Eighteen-inch tops. Made by Paul Bond Boot Company.

Underslung heels. Made by Riff Raff Leatherworks.

First pair. Made by
Deana McGuffin,
McGuffin Custom Boots;
worn by her grandson,
Ian Lewis Woodall.

Next Steps: Customizing Your Boot

Owning a pair of custom-made cowboy boots is an adventure within reach—all you need is money and patience. Prices for custom-fit boots start at six hundred dollars (a little less for a custom design in standard sizes) and go up into the thousands, depending on materials and labor.

Traveling someplace new and shaking hands with your bootmaker is much of the fun of ordering custom. Many bootmakers will supply measuring kits to out-of-town customers but can only guarantee a boot's fit if they take the measurements themselves.

ABOVE
A customer trying on boots in Alpine, Texas, in 1939. (Library of Congress, FSA-OWI Collection [LC-USF34-033198-D])

Visiting a Bootmaker

1. Make an appointment with a bootmaker. (See resource guide on page 316; updates available at www.jenniferjune.com/customboots.) Afternoon appointments are best since your feet may swell during the day.
2. Wear your most comfortable boots (or shoes) so the bootmaker can see which fit you prefer.
3. Wear clean socks and bring cash or a check for the deposit (many small shops do not take credit cards).

Designing Your Basic Boot

Think about when and where you'll wear your boots. Are they work boots? Will you wear them every day to the office? To a honky-tonk? Or only for special occasions? Giving this some thought will help you and your bootmaker pick the materials that are best suited to your needs.

When you order a pair of boots, the bootmaker will ask you to choose the following:

- Leather type and color.
- Height of the boot top.

- Heel height.
- Toe style. (Don't assume you can't wear a pointed or box toe until you talk it over with your bootmaker.)

You can leave the remaining decisions to your bootmaker, or you can continue designing your boot by selecting the stitch or inlay pattern, and details like the shape of the scallop and the pull straps.

Artistic Expression

Flip through the pages of this book; you might find color combinations and symbols that inspire you.

Some customers bring their bootmaker an idea; others bring a sketch. Be aware that just because you can draw something doesn't mean it's a ready-made boot design. Remember, boots are more like a sculpture than a painting: your eye will move across flat artwork differently than a finished boot top, and images often work best when they are simple and bold. Try squinting at your boot design and see what stands out.

Pay attention to the space around your designs. While a monogram can look great on an empty boot top, other inlay patterns like a howling coyote may look a bit odd if it's floating in blank space—it might look better with surrounding stitchwork or a bit more inlay.

Try repeating colors and shapes throughout your boot tops and vamps. When your eye sees the same cutouts, points, or curves, it helps unify the design and adds rhythm to the composition.

Consider colorful piping along the side seam and trim along the vamp; these can help frame the art on the boot top.

It's not unusual for new customers to wait weeks, months, or even years to have their boots made. Be patient, and remember that while you are waiting, your bootmaker will only improve at his or her trade.

What do Mickey Mouse, Texas, and the Dallas Cowboys have in common? Perhaps nothing more than a single fan. Custom boots should reflect the passion of their owner. Made by Cunningham's Lone Star Boots; courtesy of Shelly Cunningham.

"Ruby Whiteheart." Made by Sorrell Custom Boots; designed and worn by Karen Kohtz.

Fit to Be Called Art

Cowboy boots may have achieved icon status because of their longevity and popularity, but generations of bootmakers have succeeded in turning them into art. However, they have routinely been overlooked as an American art form. Even in many western museums, cowboy boots are exhibited as archival accessories to the celebrity of their owner, not as art in their own right. Perhaps one reason they aren't featured in the collections of more museums is because acquiring them is not easy. Many of America's finest bootmakers have wait times of two to four years. They often don't have the time or the inclination to make a boot that will merely sit on display.

Stacked leather heel.
Made by Stewart Romero;
courtesy of D. Alan Calhoun.

FINAL STITCHES

Cowboy boots have evolved over time in terms of color, stitching, and toe styles, but their importance hasn't diminished. They tell the American story through leather and thread: the America we want to be . . . A country full of wide-open spaces, individuality, opportunity, luck, chance, and adventure.

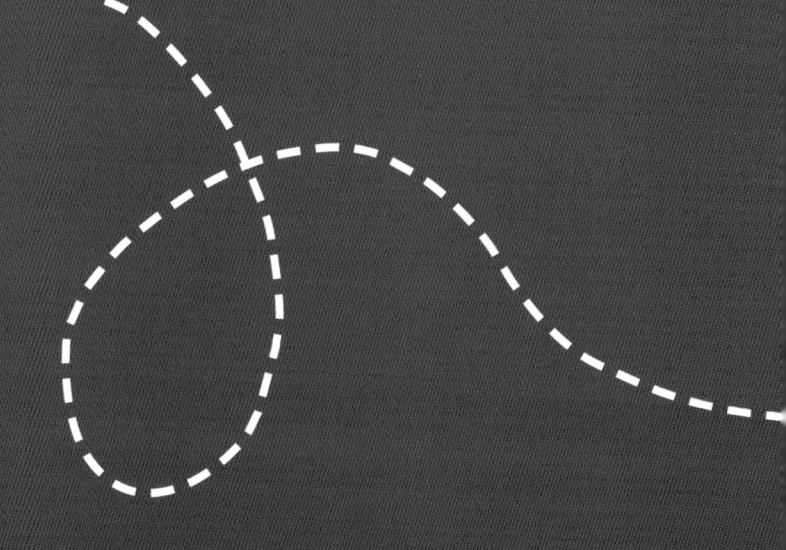

Wingtip foxing. Made by Tres Outlaws.

GLOSSARY

Bling: Popular urban slang for expensive, showy add-ons, such as silver studs, rhinestones, and conchos.

Boot jack: A tool used to remove cowboy boots while standing. The left foot is placed on the flat portion of the jack, while the right boot heel rests in the jack's V-shaped opening. A boot jack provides the needed leverage to pull the foot free. Often shaped like bugs, longhorns, and sometimes loose women, boot jacks have become popular collectibles.

Boot jewelry: Leather anklets decorated with beading and/or silver charms, worn outside the boot. These buyer add-ons can also include charms that dangle from the pull straps.

Boot tip: A decorative silver toe cap.

Box toe: A squared-off boot toe. Ordered by a horizontal measurement taken at the tip: $1/4$-inch box, $3/4$-inch, etc.

Buckaroo-style: Boots with tall tops measuring 17 to 20 inches. They are usually plain-stitched tops in bold, bright colors and sometimes have a simple brand inlay. Other common features include a broad rounded toe, pull holes, and a spur shelf.

Buck stitching: A running stitch made with a thin strip of leather lacing. Typically stitched in a contrasting color in order to outline and highlight a special piece of inlay or tooling.

Cemented sole: A sole that is glued rather than stitched, making the boot relatively lightweight. Popular with many stage performers, this single-layer sole is closely trimmed to the boot for a sleeker look.

Collar: A piece of decorative leather overlaid along the very top of a boot. Usually a collar is in a contrasting color to help frame the boot design. It often repeats the shapes and colors found elsewhere on the boot.

Conchos: Originally known as "concha," these silver buttons with wide slots are used to reinforce the lacing commonly found on saddles and chaps. Engraved conchos have become largely decorative, adding western-style glamour to boot tops and belts.

Cone: The part of a boot last that corresponds to the middle part of the foot: the arch between the toes and the ankle.

Counter: Most cowboy boots have a four-piece top. The piece of leather that surrounds the wearer's heel is called the "heel counter."

Crimping: A bootmaking step meant to take the stretch out of the leather so that a custom boot will stay true to its measurements after being worn. The wet vamp leather is pulled, nailed, and left to dry on flat boards that have the shape of Christmas stockings.

Cuban heel: A high boot heel that narrows in the middle and flares at the bottom, like a pair of bell-bottom jeans.

Foxing: Any decorative piece of leather overlaid on a boot toe or heel. It can be simple or fancy with multiple colors, cutouts, and decorative stitching.

Inlay: Shapes are cut out of a boot top, and layers of colorful leather are placed underneath. The inlays are held in place with one or more rows of stitching.

Instep: The arched part of the foot between the toes and ankle.

Lacing: Thin strips of leather that are stitched and woven by hand into decorative seams and edging.

Last: A wooden or plastic form used in bootmaking. The last reflects both the wearer's foot measurements and elements of the finished boot, such as toe shape and heel height. Custom bootmakers will build up or grind down a last until it matches a customer's exact foot measurements.

Lasting pliers: A curved pair of pliers with a small hammerhead on its backside. During bootmaking, these pliers are used to stretch the leather over the last and hammer the small tacks that hold the leather in place.

Mule ears: Long decorative boot pulls. Mule ears tend to be very long, nearly touching the ground.

Overlay: A decorative technique that adds layers of leather on top of a boot top. Overlay can be quite delicate, like filigree or scrolling, and is often combined with inlay.

Packer: A lace-up boot popular with working cowboys in the Pacific Northwest.

Pee-wees: A boot style of the 1940s and 1950s, with decorated tops that were 10 or 11 inches tall, making them easy to pull on and off.

Pegs: Tiny pieces of hard wood, tapered at one end. Pegs are used around the shank and the boot heel to attach the sole. At least two rows of pegs are found on quality boots. Expert customers turn a boot over and check its arch for the presence of pegs.

Piping: Narrow trim that runs along the boot top and side seams. Sometimes also called the "side welt." White piping is popular throughout central Texas.

Pull holes: Paired finger holes cut out of boot tops that are used in place of stitched-on pull straps. Popular with working cowboys who believe that pull straps may get caught on gear or under brush while riding.

Pull straps: Straps found at the top of the boot. A well-fitting cowboy boot won't go on the foot without some tug and pull.

Regal top: A one-piece boot top with a flat seam or lacing in back. Often used by bootmakers to avoid having side seams interrupt intricate inlay or tooled patterns.

Roper: A nickname given to short-top boots with a flat heel and rounded toe. An inexpensive work boot popularized by Justin Boots.

Rough-out: A cowboy boot with a sueded leather foot. The boot top is usually made from a smooth, often colorful leather.

Scallop: V-shaped top edge found in the front and back of most cowboy boots. This edge can be cut deep or shallow, depending on the wearer's preference. When there is no scallop, it's called a "stovepipe" top.

Shank: The narrow part of the boot sole found under the arch of the foot.

Side seam: The seam that attaches the two-piece boot top. Side seams run vertically on the inside and outside of the wearer's leg. Boot pulls often cover a portion of the seam. Contrasting piping is used to add color and complement the stitching.

Skive: A technique used to flatten the seams of a cowboy boot. Nearly all pieces used in boot tops are flipped over and their edges are thinned down (or feathered) with a razor-sharp knife.

Spur guard: An additional layer of leather stitched across the top of the wearer's foot. Designed to protect the vamp of the boot from rubbing and wear.

Spur shelf: The small ledge on the back of a stacked boot heel. Normally bootmakers tightly trim the heel to the foot of the boot, but some cowboys request a short overhang to give their spur's heel band a place to rest.

Stovepipe: A boot top with a straight top edge with no dip or scallop. Reminiscent in style to military or biker footwear.

Toe box: A stiff piece of leather or celastic, molded and shaped for the boot's desired toe style. The toe box sits between the lining and top leathers, so it is not visible to the wearer. Custom bootmakers shape each toe box individually, and matching the right and left is no easy task.

Toebug: A decorative stitch on a boot toe, most often a combination of straight horizontal lines of stitching with three or more loops. Many bootmakers choose a single toebug pattern and use it throughout their career as a sort of signature. A kind of Western fleur-de-lis, it is also called a "toe flower."

Toe cap: A decorative silver tip that covers the pointed toe of a cowboy boot.

Tongue: The peak of leather where the vamp leather meets the boot top. Some bootmakers use the same tongue pattern repeatedly as their trademark; others change its shape to complement the inlay shapes stitched elsewhere on the top.

Tooling: Ornate designs carved and stamped into leather.

Triad: A boot made with three-piece construction rather than the traditional four. In this style of boot, there is no heel counter. The boot top extends all the way to the sole, and the vamp stops inches short of the boot's side seams, giving this style the look of overlay.

Underslung: When the back of a boot heel does not angle straight down but at a forward angle towards the toe.

Vamp: The piece of leather that goes over the top of the wearer's foot. The boot toe is at one end, and the tongue is stitched to the top at the other end.

Variegated stitching: Thread that has been dyed with patches of multiple colors or with different shades of a single color.

Welt: A strip of leather that runs over the front part of a cowboy boot. While the stitches on the welt and outer sole are the only ones visible to the wearer, the welt is also stitched to the insole.

Wingtip: Fancy leather overlay on a boot toe that is similar to other "foxing" but is often bordered with a uniform row of small punched holes.

Wrinkles: Horizontal rows of stitching near the toe of the boot, often raised with cotton cording placed between the top and lining leather. After being worn, the boot leather naturally creases along these rows, creating a sleek look.

RESOURCES

WHERE TO FIND COWBOY BOOTS

There are more than two hundred talented custom bootmakers located in the United States and several others worldwide. Below are the bootmakers featured in this book and the page number(s) on which their boots appear. For a complete and current list of America's bootmakers, please visit www.jenniferjune.com/customboots, or send a self-addressed stamped envelope to Jennifer June, 3020 El Cerrito Plaza #273, El Cerrito, CA 94530.

Acme Boots (p. 120)
Division of H. H. Brown Shoe Company, Inc.
30 North Third Street
Womelsdorf, PA 19567
(610) 589-4586
www.hhbrown.com

Arditti Alligator (p. 325)
2137 East Mills Avenue
El Paso, TX 79901
(877) ARD-ITTI
www.ardittionline.com

Austin-Hall Boot Company
(p. 219)
230 Chelsea Street
El Paso, TX 79905
(915) 771-6113
www.austinhallboot.com

Back at the Ranch (pp. 72, 159, 182 *top right*, 226, 236, 328 *bottom right*)
209 East Marcy
Santa Fe, NM 87501
(505) 989-8110
www.backattheranch.com

Big Star Boots (p. 335)
By appointment only
3020 El Cerrito Plaza # 273
El Cerrito, CA 94530
(510) 435-5863
www.bigstarboots.com

Blucher Custom Boots
(p. 109 *bottom right*)
PO Box 480
Beggs, OK 74421
(918) 267-5393
www.blucherboots.com

Bob McLean Custom Bootmakers (p. 131)
40 Soldiers Pass Road
Sedona, AZ 86336
(520) 204-1211

Botas Fel-Yni (p. 144 *top*)
León, GTO. Mexico
(477) 762-2794

Brian Thomas Boots
(pp. 243, 290)
363 East South Eleventh
Abilene, TX 79602
(325) 672-2334

Buck Steiner Maker (Capitol Saddlery)
(pp. 224, 329 *top left*)
1614 Lavaca
Austin, TX 78701
(512) 478-9309
www.capitolsaddlery.com

Champion Attitude Boots/Caboots (pp. 99, 186, 332 *top*)
2100 Wyoming
El Paso, TX 79903
(915) 544-1855
www.caboots.com

Coe Custom Boots (p. 28)
PO Box 1674
Alturas, CA 96101
(530) 233-2564
www.cowgirlbootmaker.com

Cowboy Boots by George
(pp. 42, 248)
2792 Kelly-Toponce Road
Bancroft, ID 83217
(208) 648-0837
www.cowboybootsby-george.com

C. T. Boot Shop (Carl Chappell) (pp. 185, 246, 274, *front cover*)
105 South Main
Saint Jo, TX 76265
(940) 995-2901

Cunningham's Lone Star Boots (p. 305)
4606 Mimosa Lane
Wichita Falls, TX 76310
(940) 781-4505

Custom Boots by Morado
(pp. 71, 111)
402 Frisco Street
Houston, TX 77022
(713) 694-7571

Daly Boots (pp. 60, 280)
7358 Reindeer Trail
San Antonio, TX 78238
(210) 682-6668
www.dalyboots.com

Dave J. Hutchings' Boots
(pp. 20, 218)
8410 Garfield Way
Thorton, CO 80229
(303) 289-6726

Dew's Custom Handmade Boots (p. 64)
16797 CR 138W
Vernon, TX 76384
(940) 552-7247

Duck Menzies Bootmaker
(pp. 7, 59, 188, 222, 249, 255, 294 *bottom right*)
1636 West FM 93
Temple, TX 76502
(254) 933-2485

Resources

San Angelo butterfly.
Maker unknown; collection
of Mark Fletcher.

Gina C. Guy (p. 88)
320 West Thirty-seventh Street, Floor 12A
New York, NY 10018
(212) 736-9448
www.lariatgangboots.com

Gjelstein Custom Cowboy Boots (p. 56)
614 First Street South/Box 44
Brewster, WA 98812
(509) 689-2838

Glenderson Daly (SAS Shoemakers, Daly Boots) (pp. 60, 280)
7358 Reindeer Trail
San Antonio, TX 78238
(210) 682-6668
www.dalyboots.com

James Leddy Boot Company (pp. 62, 171)
1602 North Treadaway
Abilene, TX 79601
(325) 677-7811

Janet Stoddard Custom Boots (pp. 66, 86)
By appointment only
Chicago, IL 60630
(773) 685-5888

Jass Boot Shop (p. 216)
803 East Avenue G
Lampasas, TX 76550
(512) 525-4165

J. B. Hill Boot Company (p. 97)
335 North Clark Drive
El Paso, TX 79905
(915) 599-1551
www.jbhilltexas.com

Jim Babchak (pp. 238, 330 *top right*, *bottom left*)
By appointment only
Scarsdale, NY 10583
(917) 355 6903

Jim Covington (pp. 110, 148, 247, 297 *top*, 298)
418 Parker Street
Gardner, MA 01440
(978) 632-1869
www.jimmielukecovington.com

J. P.'s Custom Handmade Boots
58 East Highway 54
Camdenton, MO 65020
(573) 346-7711
www.jpsboots.com

Justin Boots (p. 45)
Ft. Worth, TX
www.justinboots.com

Kimmel Boots (pp. 94, 105, 140, 177, 206, 252, 260, 287)
2080 CR 304
Comanche, TX 76442
(325) 356-3197
www.kimmelbootcompany.com

Lariat Gang Boots & Shoes (p. 203)
320 West Thirty-Seventh Street, Floor 12A
New York, NY 10018
(212) 736-9448
www.lariatgangboots.com

Liberty Boot Company (pp. 68 *bottom left*, 78, 92, 96, 98, 109 *bottom left*, 154, 160, 162 top, 163 *top left*, *top right & bottom right*, 174 *bottom left*, 183 *bottom*, 184 *bottom*, 234)
286 Crawford Street
Toronto, Ontario M6J2V8
Canada
(416) 588-5013
www.libertybootco.com

Little's Boots (pp. 67, 83, 144 *bottom*, 145 top, 152, 156, 182 *bottom left*, 190, 212, 244, 253 *bottom*, 270, 334)
110 Division Avenue
San Antonio, TX 78214
(210) 923-2221
www.davelittleboots.com

Lonesome Ace Boot Company (p. 124)
3501-$^1/_2$ West Walsh Place
Denver, CO 80219
(303) 935-2584
www.lonesomeace.com

Lucchese Boot Company (pp. 10 *bottom left*, 30, 38, 40, 43, 207, 231, 296)
203 West Water Street
Santa Fe, NM 87501
(505) 820-1883
www.lucchese.com

Luis Jovel (pp. 46, 50)
4219 East Shields
Fresno, CA 93726
(559) 222-7091
www.luisjovelboots.com

Manuel
1922 Broadway
Nashville, TN 37205
(615) 321-5444
www.manuelamericandesigns.com

McGlasson Custom Boots (pp. 114, 135, 331 *top left*, *bottom right*)
PO Box 14903
Spokane, WA 99206
(509) 891-1756

McGuffin Custom Boots (pp. 5, 6, 121, 164, 209, 294 *top right*, 302)
1113 Nashville SW
Albuquerque, NM 87105
(505) 452-0690
www.mcguffinboots.com

Meanwhile . . . Back at the Ranch (p. 130)
710 East 146th
Glenpool, OK 74033
(918) 322-9808
www.meanwhilebackattheranch.biz

Melody's Custom Boots (pp. 5, 254)
By appointment only
El Sobrante, CA 94803
(510) 222-0685

Olsen-Stelzer Boot Company (pp. 75, 267)
114 South Main Street
Henrietta, TX 76365
(940) 538-5691
www.olsenstelzerboots.com

Paul Bond Boot Company
(pp. 70, 300)
915 West Paul Bond Drive
Nogales, AZ 85621
(520) 281-0512
www.paulbondboots.com

Richard Cook Custom Boots (p. 63)
9150 FM 1101
Seguin, TX 78155
(830) 372-4470
www.richardcookcustomboots.com

Riff Raff Leatherworks (Pascal) (pp. 48–49, 161, 210, 258, 288, 301)
By appointment only
North Hollywood, CA 91601
(818) 506-4668
www.riffraffleatherworks.com

Rocketbuster Boots (pp. 1, 8, 9, 10 *top right, bottom right*, 11 *top right*, 76, 77, 80, 89, 104, 128, 136–137, 146, 157, 163 *bottom left*, 174 *top left, bottom right*, 175 *all boots*, 176, 191, 196, 201, 205, 217, 232, 235, 237, 241, 245, 282, 294 *top left*, 329 *top right*, 330 *top left*, 332 *bottom*)
115 South Anthony
El Paso, TX 79901
(915) 541-1300
www.rocketbuster.com

Schwarz Custom Boots (p. 122)
120 South Montana
Dillon, MT 59725
(406) 683-6652

Slickfork Custom Boots (p. 261)
558 Printz Road
Arroyo Grande, CA 93420
(805) 481-4944
www.slickfork.com

Sorrell Custom Boots (pp. 68 *top left*, 109 *top left*, 127, 132, 138, 139, 213, 214, 228, 242, 295 *bottom*, 306, 328 *bottom left*, 330 *bottom right*)
217 East Oklahoma Avenue
Guthrie, OK 73044
(405) 282-5464
www.customboots.net

Spikes Custom Boots (p. 204)
1202 East Spring
Henrietta, TX 76365
(940) 538-4864

Stallion Boot Company (pp. 109 *top right*, 192, 199)
100 North Cotton Street
El Paso, TX 79901
(915) 532-6268
www.stallionboots.com

Stephanie Ferguson Custom Boots (pp. 117, 133, 225)
2112 Poe Prairie Road
Millsap, TX 76066
(817) 341-9700
www.stephanieferguson.com

Tex Robin Boots (pp. 68 *bottom right*, 151, 170, 189)
2081 Sayles Boulevard
Abilene, TX 79605
(325) 691-5700
www.texrobinboots.com

Texas Traditions Boots by Lee Miller (pp. 90, 95, 100, 107, 125, 129, 145 *bottom*, 173, 182 *bottom right*, 253 *top*, 256–257, 273, 281 *bottom*)
2222 College Avenue
Austin, TX 78704
(512) 443-4447
Also contact *Texas Traditions* for remakes of vintage patterns by Charlie Dunn (pp. 107, 173, 182 *bottom right*, 256–257, 281 *bottom*)

Tlo Lowry (p. 326)
30-B Steel Dust Avenue
Moriarty, NM 87035
(505) 832-5370

Tony Lama (p. 126)
1137 Tony Lama Street
El Paso, TX 79915
www.tonylama.com

Tres Outlaws (pp. 11 *bottom right*, 14, 53, 79, 82, 106, 172, 197, 200, 229, 230, 240, 295 *top*, 297 *bottom*, 310)
421 South Cotton Street
El Paso, TX 79901
(915) 544-2727
www.falconhead.com

Weinkauf Boots & Leatherworks (p. 112)
PO Box 291846
Kerrville, TX 78029
(830) 257-4242

Wheeler Boot Company (pp. 2, 61, 329 *bottom left*)
4115 Willowbend
Houston, TX 77025
(713) 665-0224
www.wheelerboots.com

Wild Bill's Boots (p. 69)
20 Lakeside Drive
Granby, CT 06035
(860) 844-8440

William Shanor and Julie Bonney (pp. 68 *top right*, 153)
955 Penny Drive
Ashland, OR 97520
(541) 552-0219
www.westernbootmaker.com

Young's Custom Boots (p. 179)
808 Backus
Paducah, TX 79248
(806) 492-3103

The following bootmakers have passed away or are no longer accepting custom orders. Collectors should use these names in their eBay searches, or check with knowledgeable vintage cowboy boot dealers.

Jesse Bogle, Phoenix, AZ (p. 10 *top left*); **Dixon Boot Shop**, Wichita Falls, TX (pp. 168–169); **Charlie Dunn**, Austin, TX (pp. 107, 173, 182 *bottom right*, 256–257, 281 *bottom*); **Economy Boot Shop**, San Antonio, TX (p. 108 *top left*); **Jay Griffith**, Guthrie, OK (p. 150); **Joma Boots**, location unknown (p. 147) **Hakey Boot Company**, Brady, TX (p. 174 *top right*); **Hyer Boots**, Olathe, KS (p. 328 *top left*); **Kirkendall Boot Company**, Omaha, NE (pp. 34, 142, 291); **Willie Lusk**, Lubbock, TX (p. 113); **Malcom**, Wichita Falls, TX (p. 116); **L. W. McGuffin**, Albuquerque, NM (p. 333 *top*); **Nudie's**, North Hollywood, CA (p. 198, *back cover*); **Frank Polk**, Mason, TX (p. 329 *bottom right*); **Ramirez & Sons Boot Manufacturing**, Odessa, TX (pp. 101; 259); **Jack Reed**, Burnet, TX (p. 223); **Abraham Rios/Rios Boot Company**, Raymondville, TX (p. 180, 272); **Romero**, León, GTO. Mexico (pp. 24–25); **Chris Romero**, León, GTO. Mexico (p. 155); **Stewart Romero**, Los Angeles, CA (pp. 108 *top right*, 264, 294 *bottom left*, 308); **Santa Fe**, El Paso, TX (p. 328 *top right*).

If you are looking to embellish your boots with leather tooling and silver, these skilled artists work in collaboration with a variety of bootmakers on a project-by-project basis.

LEATHER TOOLING:

Carey Blanchard (p. 258)
PO Box 63211
Nacogdoches, TX 75963

Howard Knight
3443 Baldwin Road
Stevensville, MT 59870
(406) 777-3542
www.rockingkcustomleather.com

Karla Van Horne
204 Ridgewood Road
Jasper, GA 30143
(706) 692-5536
www.purdygear.com

ENGRAVING & SILVERSMITHING:

Clint Orms (pp. 213, 214, 295 *bottom*)
229b Old Ingram Loop
PO Box 249
Ingram, TX 78025
(830) 367-7949
www.clintorms.com

The following museums have cowboy boots catalogued within their permanent collections. Call or refer to their Web sites for visitor information and details on current exhibits.

MUSEUMS:

Autry National Center Museum of the American West
4700 Western Heritage Way
Los Angeles, CA 90027
(323) 667-2000
www.autrynationalcenter.org

Bata Shoe Museum
327 Bloor Street West
Toronto, Ontario M5S1W7
Canada
(416) 979-7799
www.batashoemuseum.ca

Bob Bullock Texas State Museum
1800 North Congress Avenue
Austin, TX 78711
(512) 936-8746
www.thestoryoftexas.com

Buffalo Bill Historical Center
720 Sheridan Avenue
Cody, WY 82414
(307) 587-4771
www.bbhc.org

Country Music Hall of Fame and Museum
222 Fifth Avenue South
Nashville, TN 37203
(615) 416-2001
www.countrymusichalloffame.com

Gilcrease Museum
1400 North Gilcrease Museum Road
Tulsa, OK 74127
(918) 596-2700
www.gilcrease.org

National Cowboy and Western Heritage Museum
1700 NE Sixty-third Street
Oklahoma City, OK 73111
(405) 478-2250
www.nationalcowboy-museum.org

National Cowgirl Museum and Hall of Fame
1720 Gendy Street
Fort Worth, TX 76107
(817) 336-4475
www.cowgirl.net

Panhandle-Plains Historical Museum
West Texas A&M University
2503 Fourth Avenue
Canyon, TX 79015
(806) 656-2244

Roy Rogers & Dale Evans Museum
3950 Green Mountain
Branson, MO 65616
(417) 339-1900
www.royrogers.com/museum-index.html

Smithsonian Institute National Mall
Fourteenth Street & Constitution Avenue
Washington, DC 20560
(202) 357-2700
http://americanhistory.si.edu

Texas Ranger Hall of Fame and Museum
I-35, Exit 335B
Waco, TX 78702
(254) 750-8631
www.texasranger.org

Tom Mix Museum
721 North Delaware
Dewey, OK 74029
(918) 534-1555

Weasel Bob's Boot Museum (pp. 144, 147, 328 *top left*)
By appointment only
3930 SE Thirty-seventh Avenue
Portland, OR 97202
(503) 774-3377

Witte Museum
3801 Broadway
San Antonio, TX 78209
(210) 357-1900
www.wittemuseum.org

PAGE 328
top left: **"Phillips 66." Made by Hyer Boots for a company VIP; courtesy of Weasel Bob's Boot Museum.** *top right:* **Warrior and eagle. Vintage boot by Santa Fe; courtesy of Karen Robinson.** *bottom right:* **Tooled bucking bronco. Made by Back at the Ranch.** *bottom left:* **Morning glory. Made by Sorrell Custom Boots; courtesy of Jane Aebersold.**
PAGE 329
top left: **Charlie Dunn was the head bootmaker at Capitol Saddlery throughout the 1950s. This is probably his most famous inlay style—the "pinched" rose. Courtesy of Evan Voyles.** *top right:* **"Pony Up." Made by Rocketbuster Boots.** *bottom right:* **Most Frank Polk boots are plain, as his clients were mostly central Texas working cowboys. These inlaid eagle boots from the 1950s are a rare exception. Courtesy of Evan Voyles.** *bottom left:* **Heel overlay. Made by Wheeler Boot Company.**

PAGE 330
top left: **"Cinch." Made by Rocketbuster Boots.** *top right:* **Two-toned vamp. Made by Jim Babchak.** *bottom right:* **Great Spirit. Made by Sorrell Custom Boots.** *bottom left:* **Grubby cactus. Made by Jim Babchak.**
PAGE 331
top left: **"Bull & Barbwire." Made by McGlasson Custom Boots.** *top right:* **Vintage child's boot. Maker unknown; courtesy of Mike Hathorn.** *bottom right:* **"Buffaroses." Made by McGlasson Custom Boots.** *bottom left:* **Green tassel. Maker unknown; courtesy of Evan Voyles.**
PAGE 332
top: **Gene Autry tribute ankle boots. Made by Caboots.** *bottom:* **"Sunrise Sunset." Made by Rocketbuster Boots.**
PAGE 333
top: **Three pairs made by L.W. McGuffin.** *bottom:* **Horse and star. Rocketbuster vintage collection.**

During the 1950s, cowboy boots were popular among children because they could often wear the same styles as their parents. Maker unknown; courtesy of Mike Hathorn.

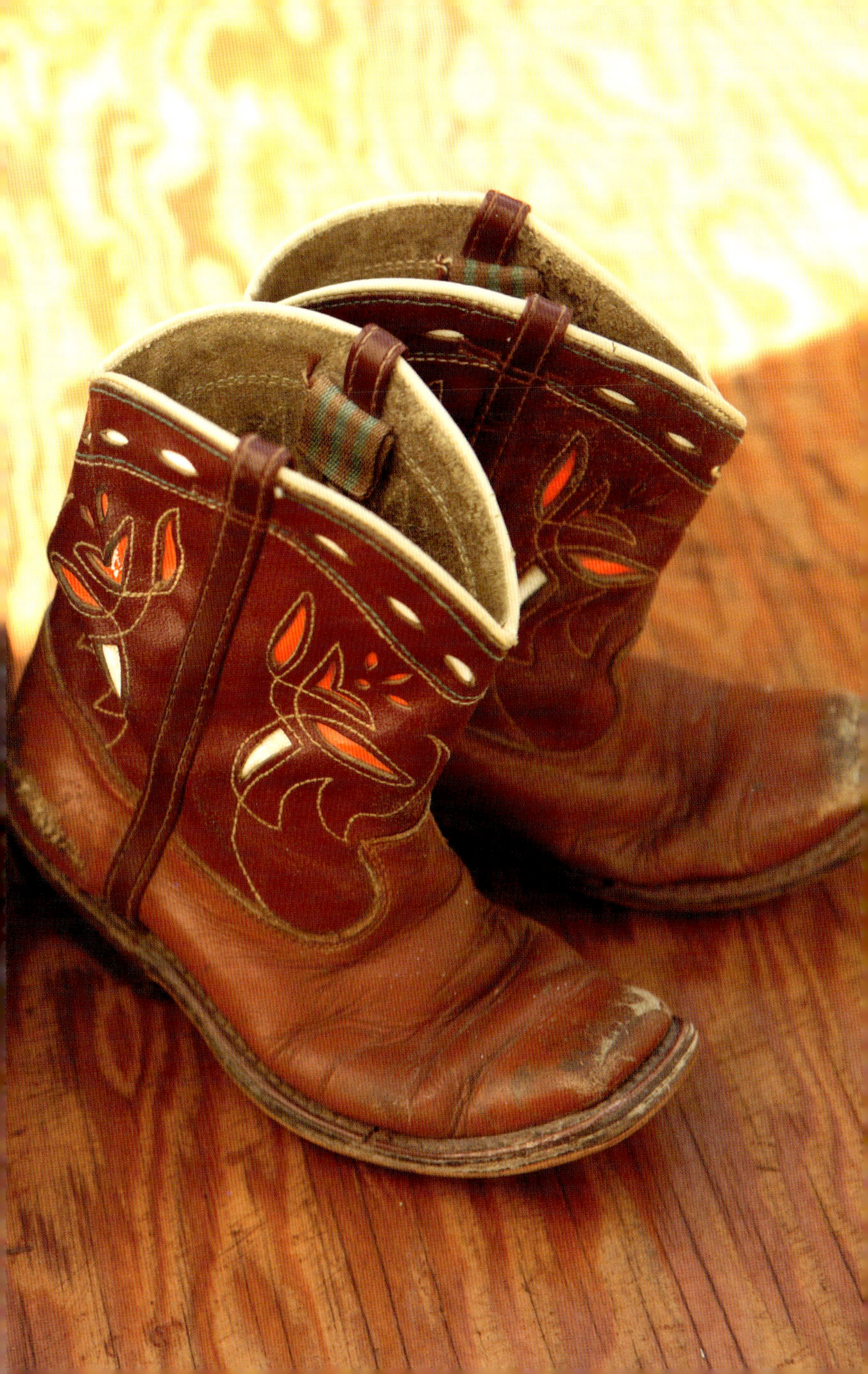

Suggested Reading

100 Years of Western Wear by Tyler Beard and Jim Arndt (Salt Lake City: Gibbs Smith, Publisher, 1993).

Art of the Boot by Tyler Beard and Jim Arndt (Salt Lake City: Gibbs Smith, Publisher, 1999).

Cowboy Boot Book by Tyler Beard and Jim Arndt (Salt Lake City: Gibbs Smith, Publisher, 1992).

Cowboy Boots by Tyler Beard and Jim Arndt (Salt Lake City: Gibbs Smith, Publisher, 2004).

The Cowboy Catalog by Sandra Kaufman (New York: Clarkson Potter, 1980).

"Day of the Dead" in *Halloween and Other Festivals of Death and Life* by Kay Turner and Pat Jasper, edited by Jack Santino (Knoxville: University of Tennessee Press, 1994).

Design Artistry by F. O. Baird (Fort Worth: The Leathercraftsman Inc., 1977).

Glamour: Fashion, Industrial Design, Architecture edited by Joseph Rosa (New Haven, CT: Yale University Press, 2004).

Hot Irons: Heraldry of the Range by Oren Arnold and John P. Hale (New York: The Macmillan Company, 1940).

How the West Was Worn by Holly George-Warren and Michelle Freedman (New York: Abrams, 2001).

The Leather Book by Anne-Laure Quilleriet (New York: Assouline, 2004).

A Lifetime with Boots by Sam Lucchese and Tad Mizwa (Houston: Cordovan, 1983).

The Longhorns by J. Frank Dobie (New York: Grosset & Dunlap, 1941).

Miss Enid: The Texas Lady Bootmaker by Enid Justin and Dale Terry (Austin: Nortex Press, 1985).

Ranch Dressing: The Story of Western Wear by M. Jean Greenlaw (New York: Lodestar, 1993).

Standard of the West: The Justin Story by Irvin Farman (Fort Worth: Texas Christian University Press, 1996).

Texas Boots by Sharon DeLano (New York: Penguin Books, 1981).

Western Bootmaking: An American Tradition by D. W. Frommer II (Redmond, OR: privately printed, 1990).

Western Shirts: A Classic American Fashion by Steven Weil and Daniel DeWeese (Salt Lake City: Gibbs Smith, Publisher, 2004).

Star status. Made by Arditti Alligator.

Filigree petals.
Made by Tlo Lowry.

Acknowledgments

Many thanks to all the bootmakers, customers, and collectors who trusted Marty and me with their wonderful and irreplaceable cowboy boots.

Special thanks to the following folks for their contributions, support, and enthusiasm:

My sweetie, Scott MacLeod; my editor, Jane Newman; Marty Snortum for the beautiful photographs; Dwight Yoakam for his kindness; Christine Knorr and Miko McGinty for the book's design; Lauren, Phil, Matt, and Alex Siegel for giving me a place to call home while in Texas; Tyler Beard and Jim Arndt for their sage advice; Evan Voyles; John Tongate; Heriberto Ibarra; Laura Neitzel; Tex Robin; Nevena Christi; Lee and Carrlyn Miller; Dave, Mary Jane, and Sharon Little; Clay Hathaway; Pascal; Dave "Hutch" Hutchings; Eddie and Kathy Kimmel; Lisa Sorrell; Brian C. Thomas; Duck Menzies; Tony Benattar; Scott Emmerich; Bob and Jackie McLean; Glenderson Daly; Stephanie Ferguson; Carl Chappell; Wendy Lane and the folks at Back at the Ranch; Jeff Borins; James Willett; Corky Dieringer; Fred King and the Lucchese Boot Company; Bruce Cole; Karen Robinson; Wayne Learned; Gary Ebbins and Anya Lorenzo at Etc., Etc. Communications; Marshall Considine; Mark Fletcher; Larry Jennings; Wayne Duncan; Howard Knight; Candace Wilhelmson at Axel's of Vail; Edward and Linda Balogh; Ann Keeler Evans; Ty R. Slyder; Sue, Howard, and little Shane Hackworth; A. J. Masaed.

I couldn't have done it without you.

—Jennifer June

This book could not have happened without all the talented bootmakers and collectors of boots who took the extra time and effort to get us their boots. Unless you have built a boot by hand, the average person has no clue how much effort goes into every pair. Most shops are small, single- or dual-person businesses with heavy workloads. On a busy day, simply boxing and shipping properly is one of the toughest things to get done. These are the people I want to thank. We couldn't have done it without you. We tried to photograph all these boots in a way that shows the extreme detail and artistry that goes into them. I hope we accomplished this goal.

—Marty Snortum

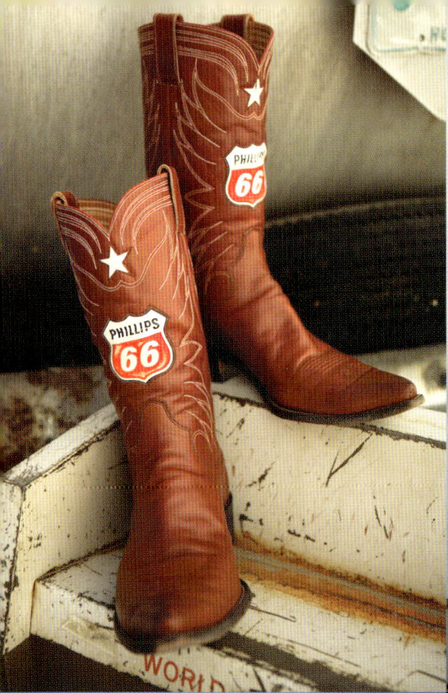
PHILLIPS
66
PHILLIPS
66
WORLD

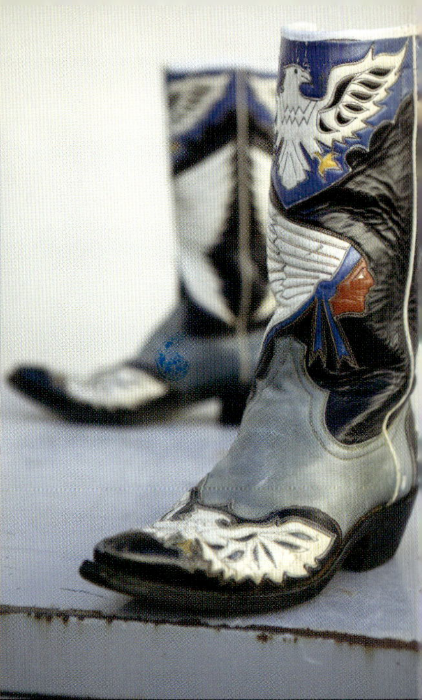

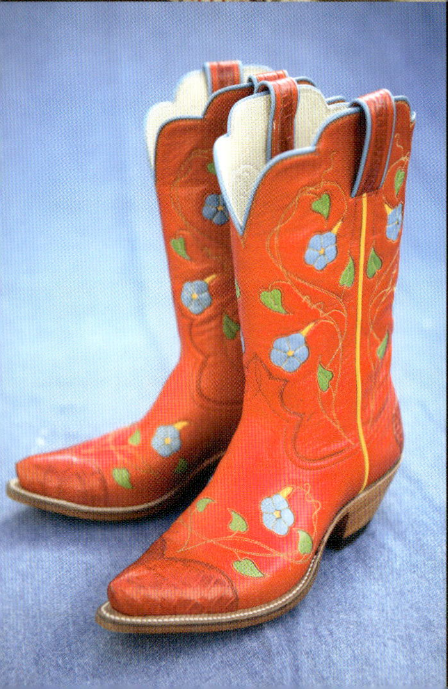

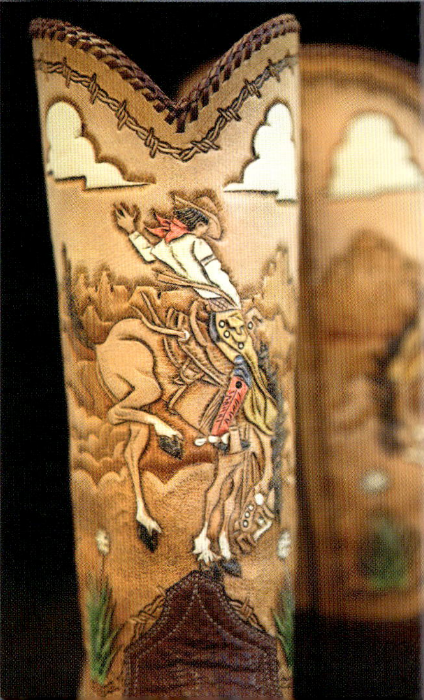

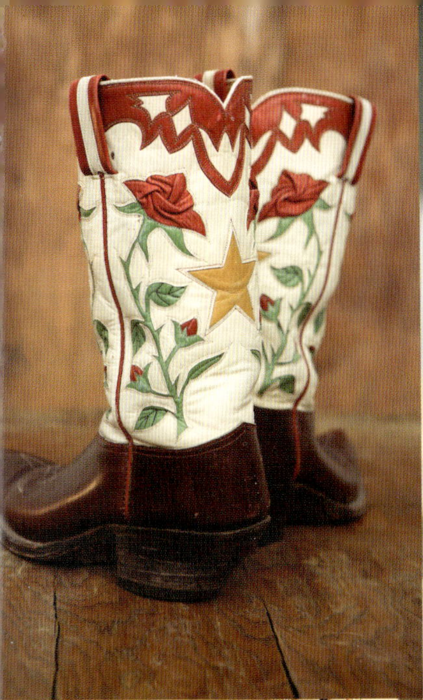

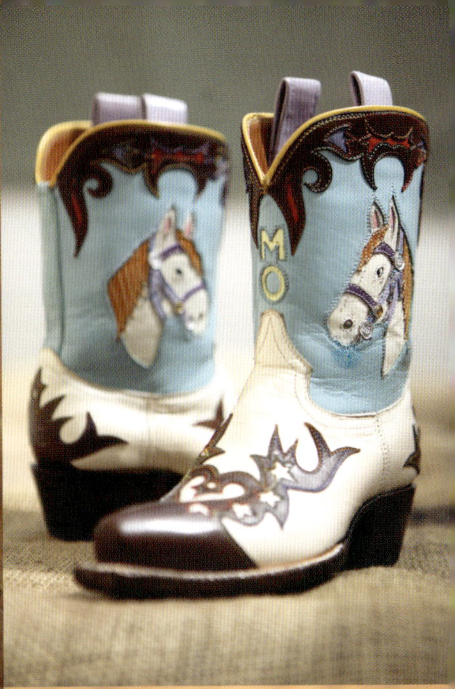
MO

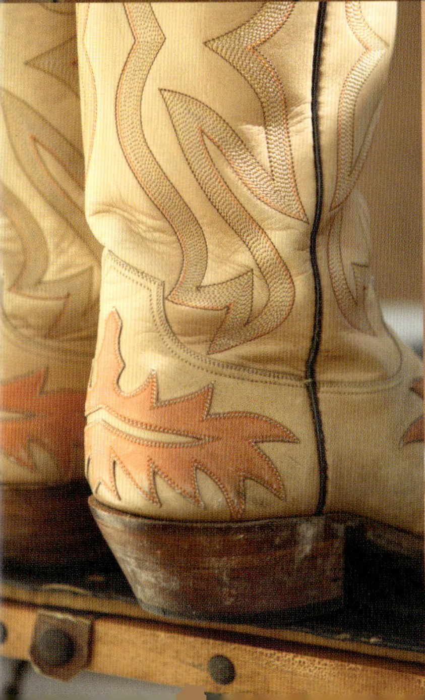

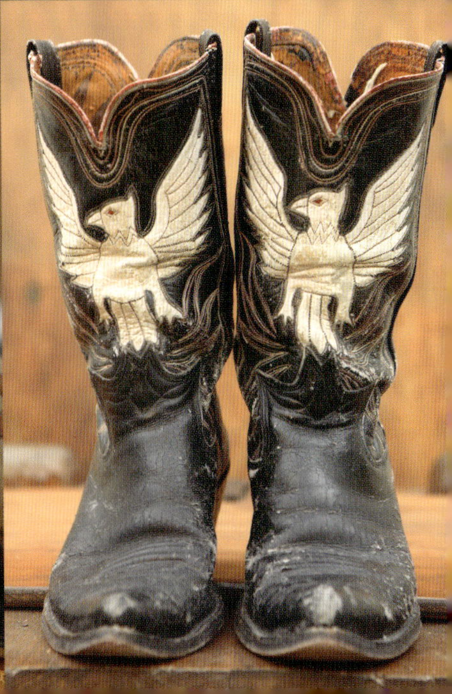

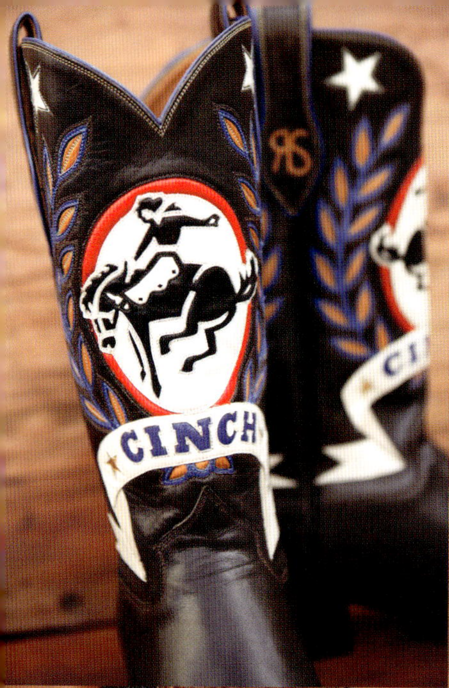
CINCH
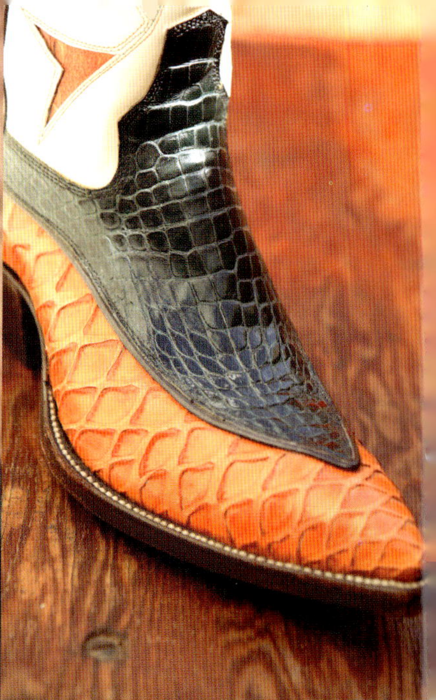
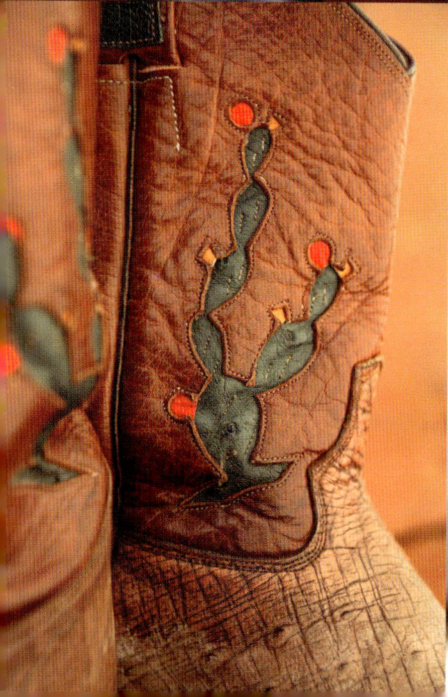
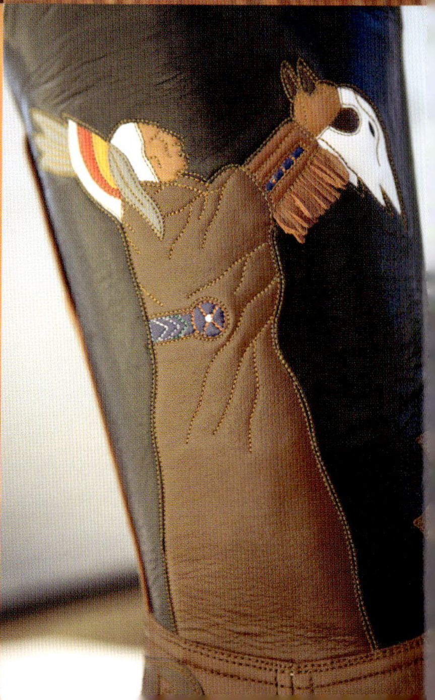

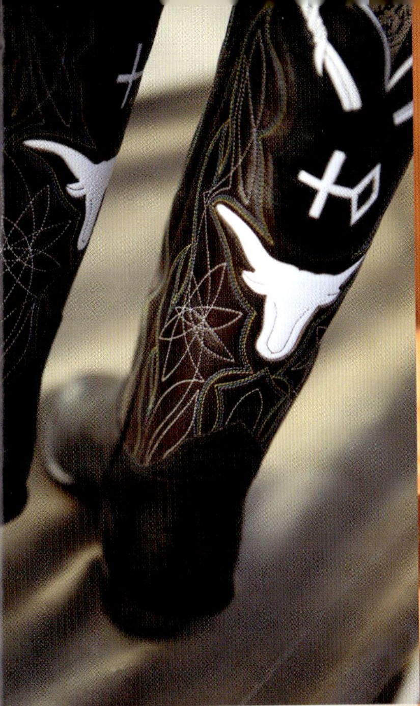
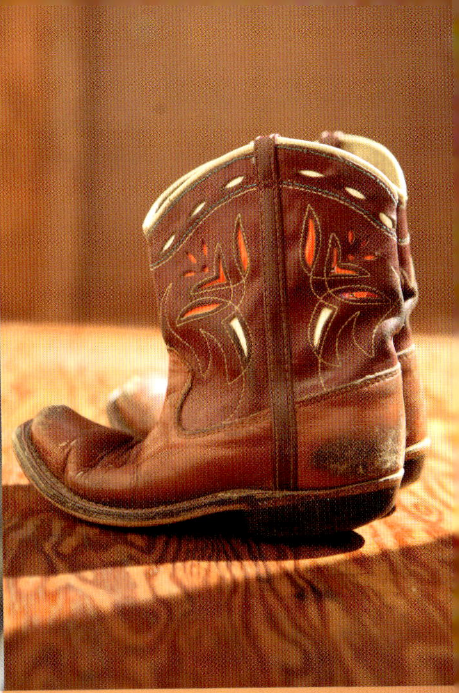
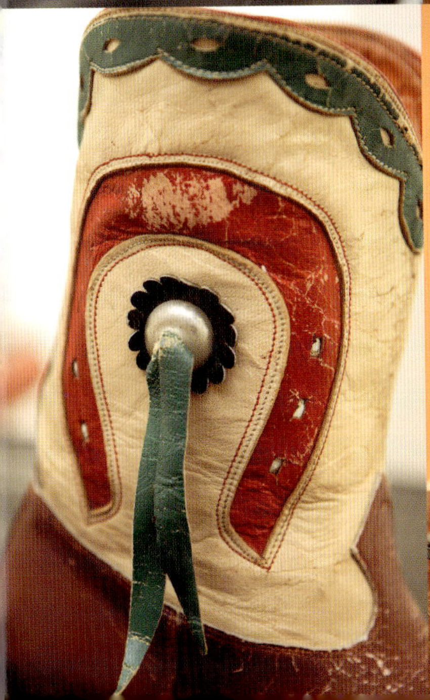
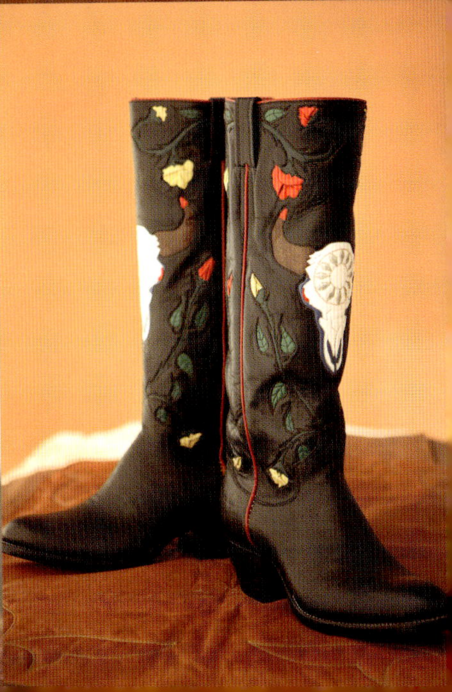

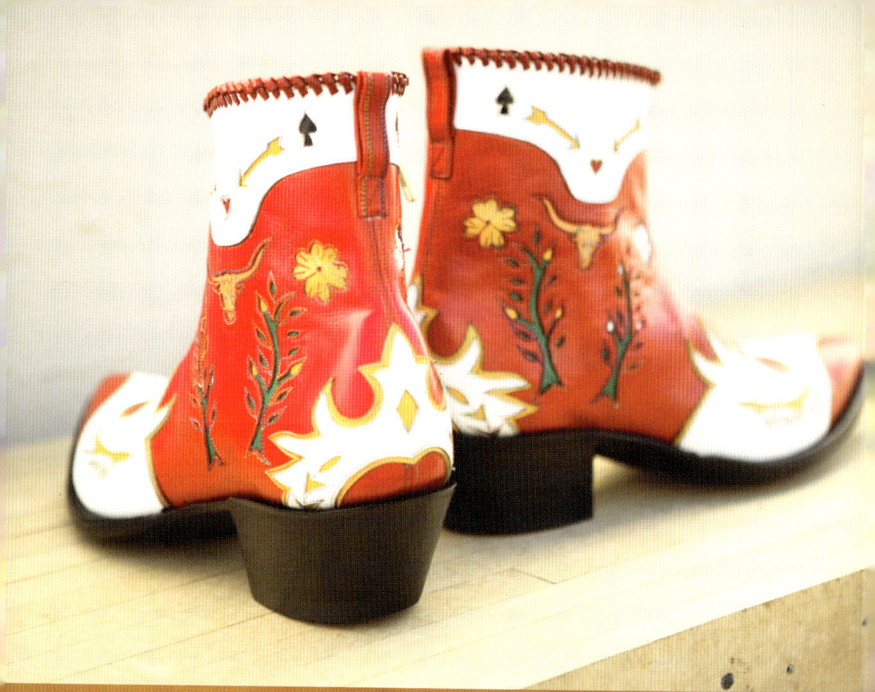

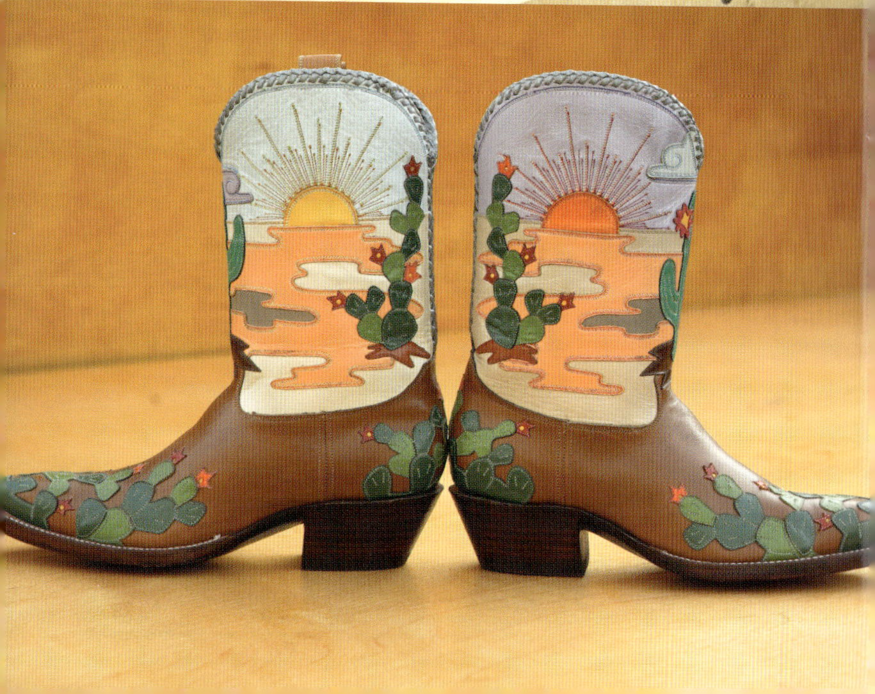

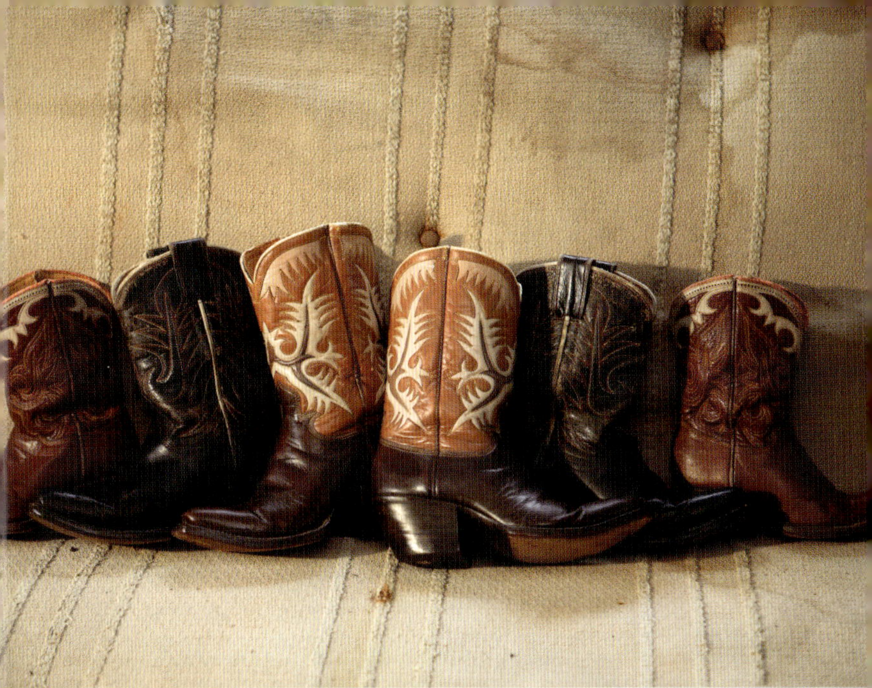

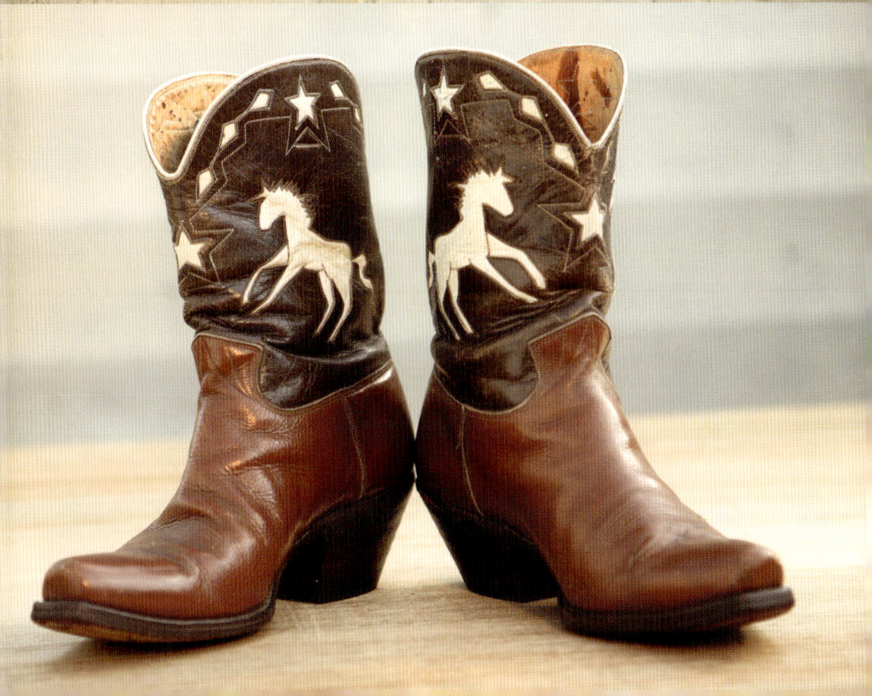

This happy-go-lucky longhorn boot top provides a wonderful contrast to the "serious" herd of cattle found on cowboy boots. Messages of wealth and good fortune are conveyed through the addition of green leather and jackpot flowers in full bloom. Made by Little's Boots.

Butterfly boots. Made by Jennifer June, Big Star Boots.

Child's boot with plastic spur. Maker unknown; courtesy of Mike Hathorn.

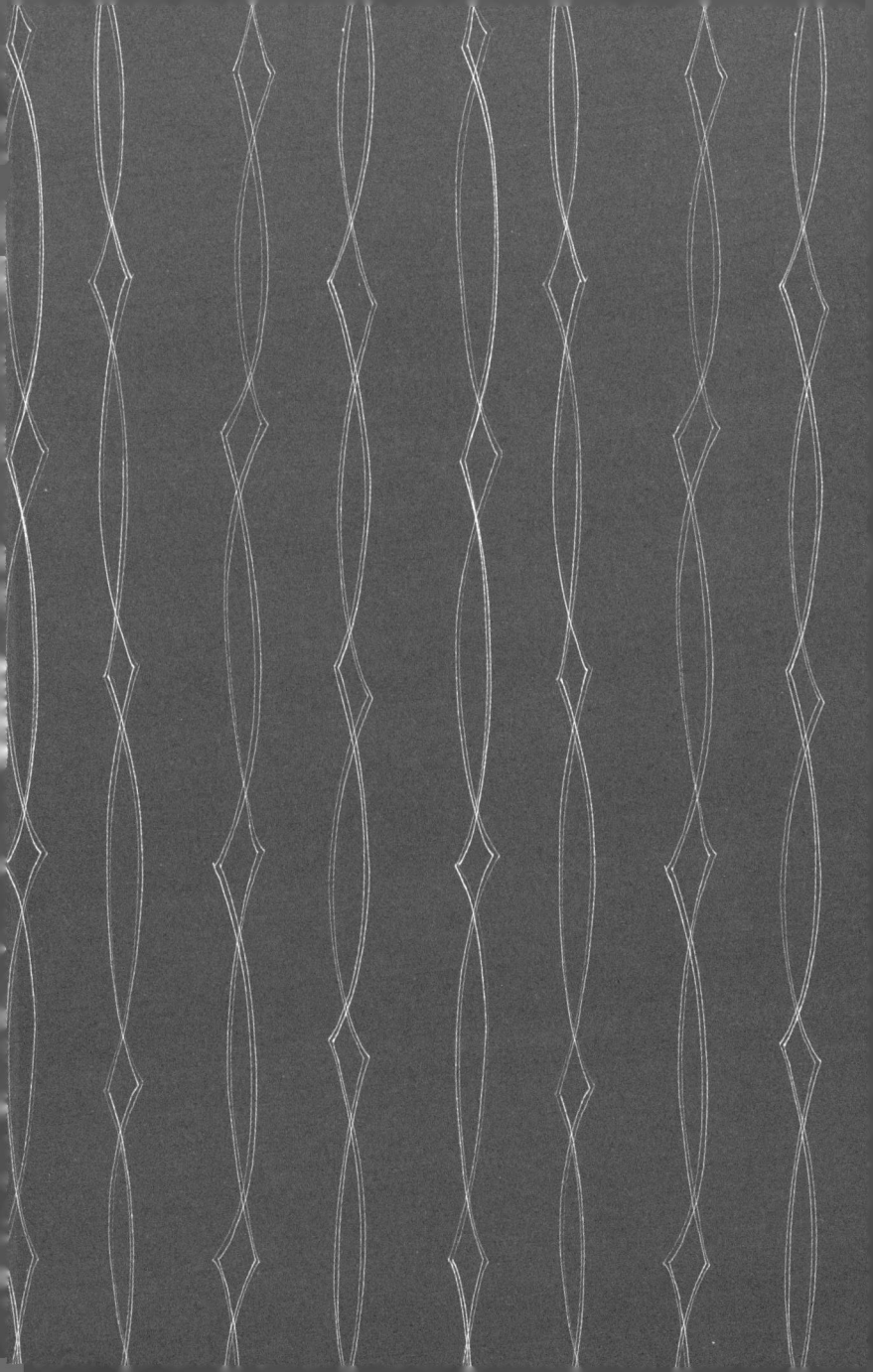

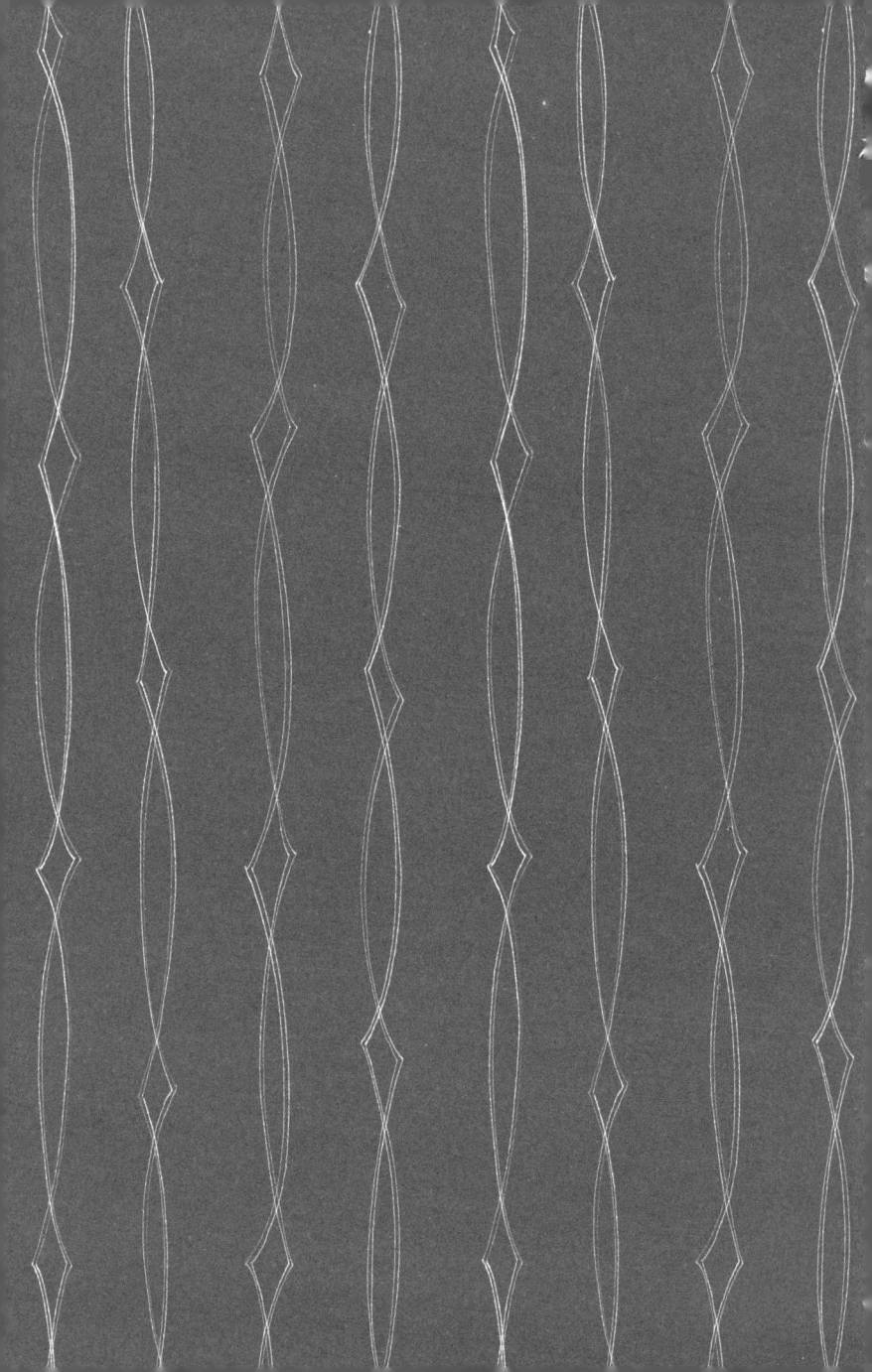